PLATO'S THOUGHT
IN THE MAKING

PLATO'S THOUGHT
IN THE MAKING

A STUDY OF THE DEVELOPMENT OF
HIS METAPHYSICS

BY

J.E.RAVEN

*Fellow of King's College and Lecturer in Classics
in the University of Cambridge*

CAMBRIDGE
AT THE UNIVERSITY PRESS
1965

PUBLISHED BY
THE SYNDICS OF THE CAMBRIDGE UNIVERSITY PRESS

Bentley House, 200 Euston Road, London, N.W. 1
American Branch; 32 East 57th Street, New York, N.Y. 10022
West African Office: P.O. Box 33, Ibadan, Nigeria

©

CAMBRIDGE UNIVERSITY PRESS

1965

Printed in Great Britain at the University Printing House, Cambridge
(Brooke Crutchley, University Printer)

LIBRARY OF CONGRESS CATALOGUE
CARD NUMBER: 65-25585

To

GEORGE RYLANDS

PREFACE

I have taken the opportunity afforded by a sabbatical year of writing this essay on the development of Plato's metaphysics, the subject of several courses of lectures or classes which I have given in Cambridge since 1950. The year happened to be the one in which Shakespeare's quatercentenary was being religiously celebrated throughout the world. My book is intended not only for undergraduates studying classics or philosophy but also for those who, like Shakespeare, have 'small Latin and less Greek': those who have largely forgotten the classics which they learnt laboriously at school; those who never read the originals but have enjoyed them in translation; those who have imbibed unconsciously, in their reading of English literature, the myths, the conceptions and the theories which ultimately sprang from ancient Greece and which, passing through diverse manifestations, interpretations and distortions, have inspired and moulded the politics, the arts and the ideals of Europe. In large measure the book is an anthology of Plato, together with the interpretations of some of his editors. The passages quoted represent, however, a personal selection and can only tell a fragmentary and incoherent story. So I have connected them with sections of commentary which vary in length and detail in proportion to the obscurity of the passage under discussion. I have neither striven to be original nor hesitated on occasions to be unorthodox or controversial. Part II in particular, which is the core of the book, contains a number of opinions that I have not read or heard elsewhere, and I might, from the specialist's point of view, have been wiser to confine my subject to three great dialogues written in Plato's middle life, the *Phaedo*, the *Symposium* and the *Republic*. Feeling, however, that the kind of reader I had in mind would like the main discussion put into its context, I decided at the outset to include Parts I and III as a purposely light frame for the picture in the centre, and later, almost as an afterthought but with the same motive, I added the Introduction.

The choice of title was difficult. The obvious solution, *Plato's Theory of Ideas*, was denied me since Sir David Ross had already written a well-known book of that name. *The Development of Plato's Metaphysics*, which would have given an accurate impression, sounded too austere and was therefore relegated to the status of subtitle. The final choice is intended not to deter the layman but still to suggest that the book makes no claim to be in any way a complete study of Platonic philosophy. Some parts of the subject, especially the central books of the *Republic* and the late dialogues, are undeniably difficult. Chapter 10 for instance, in which I have attempted, among other things, a detailed interpretation of the problematic analogy of the Divided Line, is not designed as bedside reading, while in Part III, which is meant only to tie up loose ends rather than to introduce new and specialized material, I have been drastically selective and consciously unoriginal. My purpose throughout has been to concentrate attention on the middle dialogues, because they are the ones of the greatest potential interest to the non-specialist, and I have accordingly confined my treatment of all the other dialogues to themes elaborated in that group. Any reader who would welcome a more detailed exposition of a topic on which I have scarcely touched has a mass of other books to choose from, a scanty selection of which can be found in the short bibliography.

I have included very few Greek words in the text, almost always where modern authors whom I wished to quote had already done so. Some familiar transliterations, such as Logos or Eros, have been rather reluctantly adopted as less misleading than any translation. When the meaning of a single Greek word, phrase or clause is impossible to render accurately into English, I have tried to find the nearest approximation and appended the Greek in a footnote. Occasionally also footnotes are invoked to give the original of a sentence whose translation is crucial to the interpretation of a passage. Otherwise they are reduced to a minimum.

Anybody who writes anything about Plato, especially on the basis of accumulated lecture-notes in which he may not have acknowledged every borrowing, is likely to have incurred numerous debts and forgotten some of them. So many scholars, ancient and modern, Greek and barbarian, have published their views on every conceivable aspect of Plato's thought that no student could be expected to remember where and when he first assimilated any particular notion or attitude. All conscious debts of this kind are acknowledged in the text, but there may well be as many of which I am today unaware. One debt I shall never be able to assess. During my last two years as an undergraduate I attended every lecture that Cornford gave in Cambridge and still have notes of them. Those lectures, supplemented in the intervals by reading the dialogues, imbued me with an admiration and affection for Plato which I have never lost but am constantly trying to hand on to others. I cannot estimate how many lesser debts of the same sort I may have forgotten.

Several friends and relations helped me by reading the whole or parts of the original manuscript or the subsequent typescript, and nearly all of them made valuable suggestions. I am especially indebted to four of them, F. H. Sandbach, G. S. Kirk, R. W. David and George Rylands, for ungrudging assistance in their special fields. To the last of the four, who read both manuscript and typescript and expunged some at least of the stylistic blemishes, the final product is gratefully dedicated.

J. E. R.

King's College
Cambridge

CONTENTS

xi

CHAPTER I

INTRODUCTION

One of the more startling aspects of ancient Greek philosophy is the speed of its development from infancy to maturity. Thales, the so-called 'Father of Philosophy', can be dated with greater precision than most of his immediate successors by the fact that he foretold an eclipse of the sun which happened to coincide with a battle between the Medes and the Lydians. The eclipse, according to modern calculations, occurred on 28 May 585 B.C. Two centuries later Socrates was dead, Plato was at the height of his powers, the birth of Aristotle was imminent. In those two centuries philosophy changed out of all recognition. To understand the full extent of the collective achievement of Socrates and Plato, we need to know a little about their predecessors.

The whole of European philosophy evolved, by a sequence of sharp reactions, from purely physical speculations on the ultimate nature of matter. The Milesian pioneers, Thales, Anaximander and Anaximenes, seem to have assumed without question that there was a single basic substance from which the world and everything in it was originally derived. For Thales 'all is water'; for Anaximander everything sprang, by a process of gradual separation, from a primeval unity which he called 'the Boundless'; for Anaximenes the primary form of matter is air, which by rarefaction becomes fire and by condensation becomes in succession wind, cloud, water, earth and stone. Socrates, we are told in the *Phaedo*, quickly tired of such speculation; Plato indulged in it rarely, and then, as the *Timaeus* shows, only for an ulterior motive. But fortunately for the future of philosophy it soon induced the first of the chain of reactions. The enigmatic utterances of the Ephesian Heraclitus, who had a profound if indirect influence on Plato, were provoked by his impatience with the materialism of the Milesians. And Heraclitus, unlike any of his three predecessors, can still speak for himself, since many of his opinions have been preserved in his own words. Here, in G. S. Kirk's translation, is a small selection of the most relevant fragments, which are worth quoting in full as an indication of the climate of thought prevailing at the time.

[Fr. 1] Of the Logos which is as I describe it men always prove to be uncomprehending, both before they have heard it and when once they have heard it. For, although all things happen according to this Logos, men are like people of no experience, even when they experience such words and deeds as I explain when I distinguish each thing according to its constitution and declare how it is; but the rest of men fail to notice what they do after they wake up just as they forget what they do when asleep.

[Fr. 67] God is day night, winter summer, war peace, satiety hunger; he undergoes alteration in the way that fire, when it is mixed with spices, is named according to the scent of each of them.

[Fr. 51] They do not understand how being at variance it agrees with itself: there is a back-stretched connexion, as in the bow and the lyre.

[Fr. 53] War is the father of all and king of all. . . .

[Fr. 30] This world-order did none of the gods or men make, but it always was and is and shall be: an everliving fire, kindling in measures and going out in measures.

And to this selection we should add, since Heraclitus himself may never have uttered the sentence most regularly ascribed to him to the effect that 'all things are in flux', the following brief extract from Plato's own dialogue, the *Cratylus* (402a 8):

Heraclitus somewhere says that all things are in process and nothing stays still, and likening existing things to the stream of a river he says that you would not step twice into the same river.

The first of these fragments, despite its obscurity, makes one point abundantly clear. Heraclitus claims to have made a fundamental discovery which had eluded everybody else. The nature of that discovery can be dimly discerned in the other fragments quoted. The unity of the world, so far from residing in a single basic form of matter, consists in the incessant tension, strife or war between pairs of indissoluble opposites. This tension, which is regulated by the Logos, is the cause of all things, 'father of all and king of all'. As the result of it, everything is constantly changing: day changes into night, winter into summer, war into peace, satiety into hunger. The world is uncreated and eternal; the extinction of one thing means, and has always meant, the generation or 'kindling' of something else. The cessation of change would be the end of the world. Since the world is eternal, change

3   1-2

cannot cease. And for Plato, who is said by Aristotle to have learnt the Heraclitean doctrine of universal flux from Cratylus, this incessant change disqualified the sensible world and everything in it from being the object of knowledge. That which is ceaselessly changing can be the object only of ceaselessly changing opinion.

In one of his fragments (129) Heraclitus speaks with contempt, and in the past tense, of another of the Presocratics who had a great influence on Plato:

Pythagoras, son of Mnesarchus, practised scientific enquiry beyond all other men and . . . claimed for his own a wisdom which was really dilettantism and malpractice.

Pythagoras is unfortunately one of those historical figures who become legendary almost as soon as they are dead. Socrates of course is another. All that we know of Pythagoras can be very briefly recited. An emigrant from the island of Samos, he founded at Croton, in southern Italy, a school of scientific philosophy which was at the same time a sort of religious fraternity. His cosmology seems to have differed radically from that of the Milesians in that it was concerned more with the form or structure of the world than with its mere matter. His intellectual pursuits included mathematics, harmonics and astronomy. The inspiration of Pythagoreanism was the belief that by studying and assimilating the orderliness of the universe man can himself become orderly. So the quest for scientific truth is no mere intellectual exercise; it is also a moral obligation. Moreover the soul of man is immortal, it has fallen from a primal state of innocence and bliss, but it may return thither, after a cycle of transmigrations, by regaining through contemplation its original purity. In Pythagoras science and religion, the mind and the spirit, were for once united. They were united again in Plato. That is the chief reason why Aristotle, in whom the mind always predominated, could write of Plato's philosophy, as he did in chapter VI of the first book of the *Metaphysics*, that 'in most respects it followed the Pythagoreans' but contained also 'certain peculiar features' derived from Heraclitus.

The next in the chain of reactions is that of Parmenides of Elea, who wrote, probably, during the first quarter of the fifth century B.C. and who reacted, like Heraclitus, against all his predecessors alike, but especially against the Pythagoreans. Although a relatively large proportion of his writings has survived, Parmenides, again like Heraclitus, is by no means easy to interpret. Not only did he write in uncouth hexameter verse, he also attempted to compress into that medium a subject-matter which is usually prosaic and sometimes also exceedingly obscure. Two quotations must suffice to convey something of the feeling and the objective of his extraordinary poem:

[Fr. 2] Come now, and I will tell thee—and do thou hearken and carry my word away—the only ways of enquiry that can be thought of: the one way, that it *is* and cannot not-be, is the path of Persuasion, for it attends upon Truth; the other, that it *is-not* and needs must not-be, that I tell thee is a path altogether unthinkable. For thou couldst not know that which is-not (that is impossible) nor utter it; for the same thing can be thought as can be.

[Fr. 8] One way only is left to be spoken of, that it *is*; and on this way are full many signs that what *is* is uncreated and imperishable, for it is entire, immovable and without end. It *was* not in the past, nor *shall* it be, since it *is* now, all at once, one, continuous; for what creation wilt thou seek for it? How and whence did it grow? . . . It must either completely be or be not. . . . And how could what *is* thereafter perish, and how could it come into being? For if it came into being, it *is* not, nor if it is going to be in the future. So coming into being is extinguished and perishing unimaginable. . . . But motionless within the limits of mighty bonds, it *is* without beginning or end, since coming into being and perishing have been driven far away, cast out by true belief. Abiding the same and in the same place, it rests by itself and so abides firm where it is. . . .

On the basis of such passages as these, which introduce an unprecedented form of supposedly irrefutable logic, Parmenides' own conclusions can be baldly summarized as follows. Our reason tells us that reality is one, homogeneous, eternal, changeless, motionless. If our senses seem to belie this, so much the worse for our senses. As there are two 'ways of enquiry', so there are two worlds. The world of reality or truth can be apprehended only by the reason from the premise 'It is'. The world of seeming or appearance, the unreal world apparently revealed to us by our senses, involves the combination of the true premise 'It is' with the untrue premise 'It is not'. The premise on which the opinions of mortals are based, or, as Parmenides himself puts it in Fragment 6, the 'way . . . on which mortals wander knowing nothing, two-headed' is the logically indefensible premise 'It is and it is not'.

Although Aristotle omits to mention Parmenides in his summary accounts of Plato's debts to earlier thinkers, this particular debt, especially when coupled with that to Heraclitus, is a large one. As Plato digested the doctrines of his predecessors he came to believe, as had Parmenides, in two separate or separable worlds. The world of seeming, which is itself, like everything in it, in constant flux, can never admit of more than opinion. If knowledge is to be possible at all, it must be knowledge of quite a different world, a world no less eternal, changeless and motionless than that revealed to Parmenides by the way of truth. Plato himself, unlike Aristotle, often, if obliquely, acknowledges his debt to Parmenides, not least in the dialogue named after him. And Plato is by no means the only philosopher who is thus indebted.

Presocratic philosophy ended as it had begun in physical speculation. The atomic theory of Leucippus and Democritus was its brilliant culmination. For the time being no further progress along that road was conceivable. Although he is regularly and rightly classed as a Presocratic, because almost all of his theories are physical, Democritus seems from our inconclusive evidence to have been some ten years younger than Socrates himself, who was born in 469 B.C. Anyhow, the period between Parmenides and Democritus had witnessed the next in the sequence of major reactions, the initiation and the spread of what is called the 'Sophistic Movement'. And even if the importance of this latest reaction has often been exaggerated, anybody who has read even a small fraction of Plato's dialogues will agree that, for him at least, the sophists were of greater significance than the atomists. They stimulated Socrates into a struggle to the death.

The chief problem concerning the Sophistic Movement is to determine whether it was a movement at all. In the latter half of the fifth century several individual sophists were earning their living as itinerant lecturers, eager to instruct their pupils, for an appropriate fee, in anything from politics or rhetoric to higher mathematics or literary criticism. Plato himself has left us portraits, lifelike but not on that account necessarily accurate, of a few of them, ranging from their most distinguished representatives, Protagoras and Gorgias, to the blindly self-satisfied polymath Hippias. Whether or not these individual sophists ever convened in conference to determine the basis of their creed, Socrates and Plato react towards them as if they had. Plato and the Socrates of his dialogues are together the most reliable of our witnesses on the sophists collectively, and what they tell us about the attitude to life which the sophists imparted, for a price, to their usually youthful pupils amounts in brief to this. Live according to the dictates of nature rather than convention. Convention is merely a contract into which the weak enter in the hope of depriving the strong of their natural rights. The principal right of the strong is pleasure; and rhetoric, the art of making the weaker case appear the stronger, is a useful instrument towards attaining that end. Pleasure indeed, or self-gratification, is the only criterion by which to regulate life. 'Man', as Protagoras said, 'is the measure of all things.' Good and evil, right and wrong, have no universal meaning; all our sensations and opinions can never be more than subjective; what point can there be, therefore, in pursuing anything else but our own personal pleasures?

Such was the amalgam of teaching which Socrates and Plato set out to combat. Socrates, the most single-minded of men, lived his life in deliberate and determined opposition to the sophistic ideals or lack of them. He knew, as the *Apology* tells us, that the only ideal of any value in life was 'to make your soul as good as possible'. He knew from his own experience that goodness is the only source of happiness as opposed to pleasure. He knew by instinct that there are eternally and universally valid ethical standards. Debarred from taking part in politics by his 'divine sign', whose orders were invariably negative, he passed his time in an incessant attempt to define those standards. His life was in every sense profoundly simple, because he lived for a single objective. Everything else but the quest for goodness was indifferent to him.

With Plato, as we shall see, the situation was radically different. Although in the end his devoted admiration of Socrates became the ruling influence in his life, it did so only after a long and painful struggle. For of all men who ever lived Plato must have been one of the most versatile. Even when politics and poetry had alike been renounced in favour of philosophy, the versatility is still self-evident. Plato's readers approach him to this day from different angles and with different purposes. A mass of modern literature is concerned exclusively with one or other of the many separable strands which he wove into his philosophy: his logic, his epistemology, his dialectic, his ethics, his psychology, his religion, his metaphysics, and even his political theory. His very versatility must have made life much harder for him than it had been for Socrates, whose single-mindedness was difficult to follow. His decision to set down his wide-ranging thoughts in dialogue form has teased his admirers with many problems. First, where does Socrates end and Plato begin? And even if we settle that question to our own satisfaction, then which of Plato's numerous interests was the one that led him on beyond the position of his master?

This book is, in part, yet another attempt to answer these two familiar questions. The crucial stage in Plato's philosophical development seems to fall in the period, which is of unknown duration, in which he wrote the *Protagoras*, the *Gorgias* and the *Meno*. In these three dialogues, if anywhere, we can watch Plato beginning to move away from the Socratic moorings: certain aspects of the three are therefore discussed in some detail in chapters 4 and 5. In the passage of *Metaphysics* A which has already been twice cited, Aristotle records first Plato's debt to the Pythagoreans, next his debt, through Cratylus, to Heraclitus, and then continues as follows (987 b 1, tr. H. Tredennick):

And when Socrates, disregarding the physical universe and confining his study to moral questions, sought in this sphere for the universal and was the first to concentrate upon definition, Plato followed him and assumed that the problem of definition is concerned not with any sensible thing but with entities of another kind; for the reason that there can be no general definition of sensible things which are always changing. These entities he called 'Ideas', and held that all sensible things are named after them and in virtue of their relation to them; for the plurality of things which bear the same name as the Forms exist by participation in them.

Aristotle is here writing, as usual, in a style almost as condensed as that of lecture notes. What he may have meant, and what has certainly been often believed in recent times, is that Plato, as he grew older, came to see that Socrates' search for moral universals could not after all be divorced from the earlier speculations on the nature of things, of the world and of reality. Our lives must after all be lived, and our actions performed, within the setting of the external world. We shall be fortunate if we succeed in living and acting aright without any understanding of the nature and constitution of the world around us. Platonism is essentially a metaphysical or ontological theory of nature which grew gradually out of the prior Socratic problem of how we ought to live our lives.

The question remains why Plato thought fit to write almost exclusively in dialogue form. Part of the answer, no doubt, is that quite early in his life he felt this to be the best available way to perpetuate his own vivid memory of his master, and that, having once adopted the dialogue as his medium, he became accustomed and attached to it. But there is more to it than that. The dialogue form enabled Plato to make thoughts or theories, rather than real people, the central characters. It enabled him, for instance, to take Protagoras or Gorgias on beyond the position where those actual individuals would have halted to what he saw as the logical conclusion of their incomplete or muddled thinking. In the dialogue named after Gorgias, Plato is generous enough to spare the sophist himself the final exposure and soon turns instead to rend two of his disciples. In the *Protagoras*, however, he shows no such leniency, but cunningly lures his distinguished adversary into a position which the real man would have repudiated. Plato is time and again attacking, not the individual human characters who figure in his dialogues, but the trends of opinion for which he believed them to stand. That is why his portraits of individual sophists should not be too readily accepted as historical evidence.

So to a final introductory point of some importance. The Greek language of Plato's day possesses, at one and the same time, the elusive suppleness of youth and the expressive subtlety of maturity. Both characteristics are obtrusive in the Platonic dialogues. Many crucial words of the ancient Greek language, so far from having a single basic meaning to which other secondary meanings were subsequently added, started their lives with a woolly fog of meaning from which the various separable senses were progressively condensed and crystallized. A case in point is the word Logos, which has already figured in this introduction in fragment 1 of Heraclitus. That single short word, as a lexicon will prove, came to cover a variety of meanings ranging from 'word', 'sentence', 'discourse', 'story', 'language' to 'reason' in all its senses, 'account' in all its senses, 'proportion' and 'analogy'. Plato, like any Greek writer of the time, uses the word often, and on occasions he uses it, as he does in the vitally important autobiographical speech of Socrates in the *Phaedo*, in a sense which cannot be precisely determined, let alone translated into equivalent English. And the same is true of many other words that he often uses: εἶδος, for instance, which means, among many other things, a Platonic 'Idea' or 'Form', or διάνοια, a crucial word in the central Books of the *Republic*, for which no exact English counterpart exists. In the fifth and fourth centuries B.C. the Greek language was still ill-adapted to the expression of abstract thought. Plato set about adapting it to that end. No wonder that we cannot always decide in precisely what sense we are to interpret one of these key words.

This is the chief linguistic problem confronting those who read Plato in his own language. For the translator there are further difficulties ahead. Cornford has some delightful comments on this subject in the preface to his translation of the *Republic*. For instance (p. vi):

The unfortunate effect of a too literal translation may be illustrated by some extracts from the Loeb edition:
'This then', said I, 'if haply you now understand is what you must say I then meant, by the statement that of all things that are such as to be of something those that are just themselves only are of things just themselves only, but things of a certain kind are of things of a certain kind' (438 D, vol. I, p. 393).
With the help of the context and some explanatory notes, the reader, it is true, will gather that the sense of this dark saying is as follows:
'This, then, if you understand me now, is what I meant by saying that, of two correlative terms, the one is qualified if, and only if, the other is so.'

But if he is more concerned to follow Plato's argument than to relish the simplicities of Greek idiom, he may prefer the paraphrase.

And what is true of the Loeb edition of the *Republic* is true of any literal translation of any of the dialogues. To cite another version of the *Republic*, that of A. D. Lindsay, hardly a page of it reads in the least like normal English conversation. Here is a random sample from the middle of a passage which will be quoted, in my own almost equally literal translation, in chapter 10:

'Then is not sight by its nature in this relation towards this god?'

'In what relation?'

'Neither sight itself, nor that in which it arises, which we call the eye, is the sun.'

'No, of course not.'

'But I fancy that of all the organs of the senses it is most like the sun.'

'Very much so.'

'And does it not possess the power which it has, by the sun's dispensation, as an effluence from it?'

'Certainly.'

'Then the sun is not sight, is it; but, being the cause of sight, it is seen by the same?'

'That is so,' he said. [Lindsay, p. 230.]

Englishmen rarely converse like that, not even teachers catechizing their pupils. And this particular passage brings out two of the main differences between ancient Greek conversation and its modern English counterpart.

The Greeks, in the first place, or at any rate the charac-

14

ters in Plato's dialogues, liked to develop their argument in a form such as this: 'Look at the matter in this way.' 'How?' 'Thus.' Cornford was right when he wrote (*op. cit.* p. vii) that in general 'the convention of question and answer becomes formal and frequently tedious'. This particular and favourite version of the convention has no place in normal English usage. Nor, second, has the practice of punctuating a friend's conversation with a monotonous series of words or phrases meaning simply 'Yes' or 'No'. To take another sample from Lindsay, again selected almost at random, Socrates' interlocutor is made to say, on the last line of page 300, 'That he must do'. On the following page his contributions to the dialogue amount to this:

'That is likely enough.'
'Obviously.'
'Inevitably.'
'Surely.'
'Probably.'
'Clearly.'

A translation which omits all of these will not be greatly impoverished. And incidentally, a glance at the original reveals that the Greek for 'That he must do' is the same as for 'Inevitably', that for 'Obviously' the same as for 'Clearly', that for 'That is likely enough' the same as for 'Probably'. The word for 'Yes', which is comparatively rare, does not occur on this page. What is the translator to do? Should he follow Cornford and, for the sake of the normal reader, omit almost all these interruptions? Or follow Lindsay and seek for a little variety in fidelity?

Or, to avoid any suspicion of suppression or distortion, remain faithful to the death?

These questions admit of no acceptable answer. The solution adopted in this book is a compromise. Passages in which the slightest distortion might be fatal to their interpretation are rendered as faithfully as English usage permits; sometimes perhaps even more faithfully than that. But where the general picture is clear and at least as important as the detail, translations such as Cornford's of the *Republic* or Hackforth's of the *Phaedrus* have been thankfully accepted. The most important and the most difficult task, in either kind of passage from Plato, is to determine and try to understand what he was primarily concerned to say.

PART I

CHAPTER 2

THE SOURCES

Almost everything that we can claim to know of the events of Plato's life derives, directly or indirectly, from the seventh of the thirteen letters which have been preserved from antiquity in the corpus of his writings. Several later authors, notably Diogenes Laertius, who lived in the second or third century A.D. and who drew freely on earlier sources, either wrote biographies of Plato, as they did of other leading philosophers of ancient Greece, or else included scraps of biographical information in works on other topics. But all that they tell us, however useful as a source of material for the romantic historical novelist, is of very little value to the historian. A few solid facts may perhaps be gleaned from them, facts such as would have become common knowledge about any great man during his lifetime and which would naturally have been handed down after his death. But they tell us almost nothing that we should be justified in accepting as historical. They embroider in an anecdotal manner on the contents of *Epistle* VII, they fill the long lacunae which that letter leaves in Plato's life with a narrative based probably on mere surmise, and they eventually convince the serious student that if he wants to learn anything certain about Plato the man, or the course of Plato's life, he should look for it only in the collected works of Plato himself, including the autobiographical *Epistle* VII.

So we come immediately to a formidable hurdle. Of the thirteen letters ascribed from ancient times to Plato, how many, if indeed any, did Plato himself write? No scholar would deny that, partly perhaps for the purpose of making some easy money from credulous librarians, the output of forged literature in antiquity, from the fourth century B.C. onwards, was immense; or that letters in particular, being of variable length and substance, are the easiest of all literary forgeries to compose and sell. If challenged on the grounds of either style or content, the forger could reply that in a personal document never intended for publication a famous writer may well have abandoned both the diction and the ethos which he took the greatest care in his published works to present to the outside world.

The history of these thirteen letters can be briefly told; the details of the story, though fascinating in themselves as a commentary on the progress of classical scholarship, are irrelevant to the thesis of this book. Not long after the beginning of the Christian era, and perhaps even earlier, the collected works ascribed to Plato, thirty-six in all, had been divided into nine tetralogies, the last of which contained, as the equivalent of a single work, a collection of thirteen *Epistles* which are presumably those that we still possess. Indeed, according to Diogenes Laertius (III, 61–2), an even earlier arrangement into trilogies by the third-century scholar Aristophanes of Byzantium had already included the *Epistles*, but in this case there is no conclusive evidence to show that the letters are the same as our present collection. Nor of course does the inclusion of the thirteen letters in one of the later tetralogies do anything to prove their genuineness; three tetralogies contain one dialogue which is now almost universally regarded as not Plato's work, while one other, the fourth, consists entirely of dialogues which are probably not his. What seems certain, however, is that in antiquity most of the letters were generally taken without question as authentic. Cicero, for instance, quotes from four of them, and incidentally writes with great admiration of the seventh, while Plutarch drew on them extensively and with no apparent doubts of their authenticity.

In modern times opinion has fluctuated. In the nineteenth century the majority of serious scholars seem to have viewed most if not all of the *Epistles* with suspicion. Zeller for example had no hesitation in rejecting even the seventh, which he admitted to be 'the most important for the history of Plato's life', while all the rest he dismissed curtly as 'quite worthless as historical evidence'. Partly, however, as the result of the acceptance by the great Wilamowitz of at least *Epistles* VI, VII and VIII, the prevailing fashion changed so much in the next half-century or so that Taylor felt justified in writing (*Plato: The Man and his Work*, p. 15): 'As for the *Epistles*, it is not necessary to argue the case for their genuineness as elaborately as one would have had to do some years ago', and he goes on to accept them all 'with the exception of I and *possibly* XII'. Yet even Taylor, great scholar as he was, illustrates one of the weaknesses which have invalidated so much of the modern debate when he writes a page earlier: 'If the *Epistles* are spurious, we lose our one direct source of information for any part of Plato's biography, and also the source of most of our knowledge of Sicilian affairs from 357 to 354.' That kind of argument surely has no validity whatever; it leads to the type of special pleading admirably exemplified by the following sentence from L. A. Post's defence of *Epistle* II (*Thirteen Epistles of Plato*, p. 25): 'A strong argument for the genuineness of the letter is the fact that it throws a great deal of light on a particular stage in the relations of Plato and Dionysius that is not illuminated by the other letters.' Precisely that consideration might well have occurred to an intelligent forger. During the last century the very same arguments have been repeatedly used by both parties as eloquent indications of either the genuineness or the spuriousness of any or all of the letters, and most of all the seventh. Unfortunately the obvious desirability of establishing *Epistle* VII as a reliable historical source weakens the force of many of the arguments used in its favour.

Epistle VII is a very curious document. Whether or not it was written by Plato, and despite the fact that it is in letter form, there can be no doubt that it was intended for publication. What it purports to be is an answer to an appeal for advice from the followers of Dion, brother-in-law of the younger Dionysius, tyrant of Syracuse, after Dion himself had been murdered in 354 B.C. by one of his own closest associates, an Athenian named Callippus. What it actually amounts to is a defence of Plato's own life, and especially of his activities during his three separate visits to the Syracusan court. I shall be quoting extensively from it in chapters 3 and 12 and will not anticipate the details of its content. But its use as a historical source must be justified now.

Although forgery was common in ancient times, all Greek letters need not on that account fall under suspicion, as some scholars seem to suggest. Of course the ancient Greeks wrote letters and naturally some of them have been preserved. And what is more, there is at least one publication of the same period, the *Antidosis* of Isocrates, which, though in the form of what he calls a 'discourse' rather than a letter, contains, just like *Epistle* VII, an *apologia* for its author's life's work. Nobody seems to doubt the authenticity of the *Antidosis*; there is therefore no ground so far for suspecting *Epistle* VII. The two works may indeed, as Post suggests (*op. cit.* p. 58), 'have a more than accidental similarity of purpose', since Plato and Isocrates were heads of rival establishments. On the other hand this argument, like almost all the rest, works both ways. Might not the pre-existence of the *Antidosis* have inspired an intelligent forger to produce a spurious counterblast?

Those critics who reject *Epistle* VII argue that, while its professed object is to give advice to Dion's party, the advice, when it comes, is so brief and trite as to be valueless. A man of Plato's stature, they claim, would have disdained such platitude. Nor, again, could he have written so discursively and with so many prolonged and irrelevant digressions. *Epistle* VII is not only unworthy of Plato, it is plainly the work of a man who, however familiar with Plato's genuine writings, is incautious in his plagiarisms, muddle-headed, and in every other respect far below the standard of Plato's intelligence. Not at all, replies the defence; if the letter were written, as it claims to have been written, in or about 354 B.C., then Plato was already, as was Isocrates when he wrote the *Antidosis*, an old man; he might well have lost some of his grip. Digressions, moreover, were always characteristic of him; are not the central books of the *Republic*, which many students would regard as the most powerful pages that Plato ever wrote, an acknowledged digression from his professed theme? And if there are details in the occasional recommendations which he makes in *Epistle* VII which seem to disaccord with the constitution that he lays down in the *Laws*, this again is evidence of a treacherous memory and a failing grasp of detail rather than of the spuriousness of an indispensable source-book. Such blemishes are exactly those which a good forger—and if *Epistle* VII is indeed a forgery, it is the work of a skilful artist—would be at pains to avoid.

The strictly linguistic discussion has followed much the same lines. For the best part of a century strenuous efforts have been made to find some linguistic criterion, such as verbal echoes from Plato's genuine works, the tolerance or avoidance of hiatus, the use of particles and the vocabulary in general, with special reference to rare words, which might enable us to distinguish the genuine letters, if any, from the false. Besides the several German scholars who tried to tackle the problem, one British scholar at least, Lewis Campbell, made a very important contribution. By a detailed study of the changes in Plato's style as he grew older, Campbell first established the now obvious point that the letters, nearly all purporting to have been written late in Plato's life, ought to reveal linguistic affinities with the late dialogues, such as the *Sophist*, the *Statesman* and above all the *Laws*, rather than with the early or middle groups. On this criterion, which effectually revealed the weakness of some of the earlier attacks upon the *Epistles*, the question once again remains open and every opinion must be to some extent subjective. A particular verbal echo from the *Phaedo* strikes one modern scholar as so inapposite in its context in *Epistle* VII as to be proof of plagiarism; others easily suppose that this particular phrase remained a favourite of Plato's till the end of his life. And every other criterion yet invented, especially perhaps that of the use of rare (rather than common) words, has proved to be equally two-edged and inconclusive. Pending some further technique or new discovery, all that can be said on the question of the authenticity of *Epistle* VII is that its opponents, linguistic as well as historical, have not yet produced a completely convincing argument. In view of the majority opinion, in both ancient and modern times, in favour of this particular letter, the burden of proof still rests with the opposition.

The authenticity of *Epistle* VII is, however, less important from my point of view than might be supposed. Even its most rabid opponents will usually admit that, if it is not Plato's own work, a member of the Academy must have written it soon after Plato's death. In that case it was still intended for publication as a defence, urgently needed perhaps by the Academy, of Plato's intrusion into

Sicilian affairs. And in that case again, any major mis-representation of the course of events would be so rapidly exposed as to do more harm than good. My own opinion of *Epistle* VII (no less subjective than another's) is that it is too discursive and digressive, and at the same time too characteristic of Plato, to be the work of anybody else. If a conclusive proof of its spuriousness were to be forth-coming tomorrow, I should be saddened but not shattered. What would undermine the whole of this book would be a proof that the events narrated in the letter never took place.

Despite the warnings of distinguished scholars, I still believe that it is possible to connect the narrative of *Epistle* VII both with the results of stylometric investiga-tions into the order in which Plato's dialogues were composed and, which is even more important, with the internal evidence on the development of his thought, in such a way that the composite picture emerging from these three separate lines of inquiry is virtually irresistible. That at any rate is what this book attempts to show.

CHAPTER 3

PLATO'S EARLY LIFE

Plato was an aristocrat by birth as well as by temperament.
His father Aristo is said to have traced his lineage back to
the old kings of Athens and thence to the god Poseidon;
his mother Perictione was descended from Dropides who,
as Plato himself tells us in the *Timaeus* (20e), was 'a relative and close friend' of Solon. She was sister of the
politician Charmides, protagonist in Plato's dialogue of
that name, and a cousin of Critias, one of the two ablest
and most influential members of the short-lived oligarchy,
the so-called Thirty, which was set up after the collapse
of Athens in 404–3 B.C. She had already had two sons,
Adeimantus and Glaucon, the young and eager interlocutors of the *Republic*, before Plato was born, and there
was also a daughter named Potone. Aristo died while
Plato was still a boy and Perictione then married her
own uncle Pyrilampes, by whom she had another son,
Antiphon. Plato tells us, in the introduction to the *Parmenides*, that Antiphon 'nowadays takes after his grand-
father of the same name and devotes most of his time to
horses'. Like many another aristocratic family, that into
which Plato was born evidently embraced a variety of
interests ranging from philosophy through politics to polo.

Plato himself was born in 428–7 B.C., a year after the
death of Pericles. His youth falls therefore in a period of
the utmost unrest and, for Athens at least, deepening

gloom. As a sensitive boy of about fifteen he must have
realized something of the horror of the final defeat of the
expedition against Syracuse. Then followed the grim
final phase of the Peloponnesian war, culminating, when
Plato was twenty-three, in the battle of Aegospotami and
the inevitable surrender of Athens. Plato came from a
family which had long played a leading part in Athenian
politics and his close relations were still doing so. The
whole of his youth must have been overshadowed by the
appalling course of events. No wonder that he found the
conversation of Socrates, with its humorous but earnest
stress on eternal values and truths, an irresistible distrac-
tion from the anxieties of daily life. Although his biographers tell us that he became a disciple of Socrates only
at the age of about eighteen, he had almost certainly
known him from his earliest childhood; both his uncle
Charmides and his cousin Critias had been close friends
of Socrates before Plato was born. But be that as it may,
there is no doubt at all that around the age of twenty
Plato conceived for Socrates an affection and admiration
which remained the ruling influence in his whole life.

Epistle VII takes up the story at about this stage in Plato's
career. The passage in question, which is so vivid that it
deserves quotation in full, starts at 324 b 8, less than twenty
lines after the beginning of the whole letter:[1]

When I was young, I had the same experience as many another: I thought that, as soon as I became my own master, I
should enter on a political career. And certain circumstances

[1] The translation of this passage is based on that of F. M. Cornford
in the introduction to *The Republic of Plato*.

in the affairs of Athens favoured this intention. The existing government was generally unpopular and there was a revolution. Fifty-one men set themselves up as a revolutionary government, eleven in Athens and ten in the Peiraeus—each of these groups to administer the market and other civic affairs—while thirty were set up as supreme rulers. Some of these were relatives and friends of mine and they immediately invited me to join them as if that were my appropriate course. My feelings were not surprising in one so young: I imagined that their administration would bring the city from an unjust way of life to a just and so I watched attentively to see what they would do.

In a short while I saw these men make the previous constitution look like a golden age. In particular, they sent my elderly friend Socrates, whom I should not hesitate to call the most righteous man then living, with various others to arrest one of the citizens forcibly for summary execution. They hoped no doubt to involve Socrates, with or without his consent, in their doings. But Socrates refused; he preferred to face any danger rather than become a partner in their unholy activities. Seeing all this and other significant things of the same sort, I was disgusted and withdrew myself from the evils of the time.

Not long afterwards the Thirty fell and the whole constitution changed. Once again, though this time less strongly, I felt the attraction of taking a public part in politics. In these disturbed times much was still going on to arouse one's disgust, and it was not at all surprising that during the revolution some took drastic revenge on their enemies; but on the whole the returning exiles showed great moderation. Unfortunately, however, some of those in power brought this same friend of mine, Socrates, to trial on a most scandalous charge, the least appropriate to Socrates of all men; they prosecuted him for impiety, he was condemned and put to death—the very man who had earlier refused to have any part in the infamous arrest of one of their own friends when they themselves were in exile and misfortune.

When I considered this, and the men who were active in politics, and made a closer study as I grew older of law and custom, the harder it seemed to me to administer the state rightly. For one thing it was impossible to act without friends and trustworthy associates, and these it was not easy to find at hand now that the city was no longer administered by the manners and institutions of our fathers; nor was it possible to make new associates with any ease. At the same time the whole fabric of law and custom was going from bad to worse at an amazing rate. The result was that I, who had at first been full of eagerness to take part in public affairs, as I watched all this happening and saw the total confusion, eventually felt quite giddy. I did not cease to consider in what possible way all these things might be improved, including indeed the whole constitution; all the time I was waiting for the right moment for action. But in the end I saw clearly that in the case of all existing states their government is without exception bad. Their systems are virtually incurable without a combination of inspired planning and good fortune. I was forced to assert, in praise of genuine philosophy, that only from that standpoint was it possible to get a true view of public and private right, and that accordingly the human race would never have respite from its troubles until either the true and genuine philosophers gain political control or else those who are already governing in the states become, by some divine dispensation, real philosophers.

It was with this conviction that I first went to Italy and Sicily . . . .

Whoever penned this passage contrived in a mere two pages or so to cover almost twenty years of Plato's life. The revolution of the Thirty, the first historical event referred to, took place when Plato was in his early twenties;

his first visit to the West was not until he was already forty. Inevitably many gaps have to be filled, and we must at this point turn to our other sources of information, particularly, as usual, the unreliable biographical tradition and such scraps of internal evidence as we can sift from Plato's own dialogues. These other sources incline me to believe that Plato himself must have written the passage just quoted. If it is the work of a forger, that forger must have given a great deal more thought and labour to his work than was customary with forgers of the period. Not only must he have read much of Plato's later prose, to familiarize himself with the vocabulary and style; he must also have pondered the early works before he could fit them into so plausible a framework.

The relevant facts or figments to be extracted from the biographers are few and far between. The most important of them are summarized by Diogenes Laertius (III, 6) as follows:

Then [that is, soon after the execution of Socrates], at the age of twenty-eight, according to Hermodorus, he withdrew to Megara, with other followers of Socrates, to join Eucleides. Next he moved to Cyrene to visit Theodorus the mathematician, and from there he went to Italy to see the Pythagoreans Philolaus and Eurytus. Thence on to Egypt. . . . (7) When he returned to Athens he lived in the Academy.

To cut a long story short, the first sentence of this passage may perhaps be founded on fact. The members of the Socratic circle, which had, after all, included notorious characters like Alcibiades, could well have felt, after Socrates' execution, that they were the object of such

suspicion that it would be prudent for a time to withdraw
from Athens. It is even possible that when, at the end of
the second paragraph of the passage quoted above from
Epistle VII, Plato or his impersonator wrote, 'I was disgusted and withdrew myself from the evils of the time',
he was referring to such a withdrawal. This view has
been held. It seems more likely, however, since this sentence comes well before the account of Socrates' execution, that he meant only that he severed his connections
with his relatives and friends among the Thirty. All that
can be said with any confidence about this part of the
tradition is, first, that Hermodorus, from whom Diogenes claims to derive it, was a pupil of Plato himself at
the Academy and so presumably a relatively reliable
source; and second that, according to Plato's own account
in the *Phaedo*, Eucleides was one of the five foreigners
present at Socrates' death and was quite likely therefore to
have offered asylum, if and when it was needed, to other
friends of Socrates from Athens.

The remainder of Diogenes' account is much more
dubious. None of it rests on the authority of Hermodorus.
The clear statement in *Epistle* VII that Plato visited Italy
and Sicily for the first time when he was about forty
years old (324 a 6) seems to dispose of the tradition that he
had already been to Italy to see Philolaus and Eurytus; the
visit to Egypt could easily be no more than a conjecture
based on certain remarks in the *Laws* about Egyptian culture and customs. The natural inference from the language of the passage quoted from *Epistle* VII is that Plato,
if not actually in Athens for most of the time, was at any

rate not so far distant as to deny him a close watch. And finally, if Plato had really travelled during this period, why does he never give us any indication of that fact? I shall suggest later that he must have been fully preoccupied after Socrates' death with concerns quite other than pilgrimages to mathematicians.

The brief last sentence in the excerpt from Diogenes is included for one purpose only: to point out that there is no suggestion that at this early stage in his career Plato had already founded a philosophical school. Diogenes' own account of the foundation, which is based on conflicting traditions, vague and almost worthless, does not come till considerably later in his essay (III, 20). The one and only suggestion of the slightest reliability to emerge from Diogenes' entire account of the events of the first half of Plato's life is that at the age of twenty-eight Plato withdrew to Megara, with others of the Socratic circle, and stayed there for an unspecified length of time. This is not contradicted by anything explicit in *Epistle* VII and it at least purports to rest on a fairly dependable authority. But even if true, it is not a fact of startling significance.

And so, with little yet established, we must turn to the third and last of our sources, the internal evidence to be derived from the Platonic dialogues. Here our first witnesses are the students of stylometry, who, on the basis of a few simple facts, such as that told us by Aristotle in his *Politics* that the *Laws* is, as we should anyhow suppose, later than the *Republic*, have made so exhaustive a study of the development of Plato's style that one of them, Lutoslawski, seems to have believed that he could determine the whole order of composition of the dialogues. Though there is general agreement in these days that such definite and detailed results should be viewed with caution, and though there is still room for wide divergencies of opinion on such important questions as, for instance, the relative dates of the *Protagoras*, the *Gorgias* and the *Meno*, yet nobody, so far as I know, would deny that stylometry has indeed established a great deal. Even Shorey, who, in his two books, *The Unity of Plato's Thought* and *What Plato Said*, castigates the sort of enquiry on which we have now embarked, still has to admit, while not himself endorsing it, that

there is now general agreement upon the broad division into three groups: the earlier, minor, 'Socratic' dialogues; the artistic masterpieces of Plato's maturity; the less dramatic and more technical works of his old age. It is generally agreed that the dramatic, minor, tentative, 'Socratic' dialogues are for the most part early; that the *Laws* is the latest of Plato's works; that the more arid, undramatic, dogmatic, elaborately metaphysical, dialectical dialogues form a later group preceding or perhaps partly contemporary with the composition of the *Laws*; and that such artistic masterpieces as the *Symposium*, the *Phaedo*, the *Phaedrus* and the *Republic* belong to the period of Plato's full maturity. [*What Plato Said*, p. 58.]

The general agreement, here twice acknowledged by an opponent, was largely the result of stylometry. But it comes in part also from the consideration, again rejected by Shorey, that the approximate order of the dialogues suggested by stylistic changes coincides to a remarkable extent with the apparent development and increasing elaboration of certain characteristically Platonic doctrines.

The first of the three 'generally agreed' groups is a large one, comprising at least nine dialogues in addition to the *Apology*, probably one or two others and perhaps also, though this is a controversial question to be considered in greater detail later, three more. I am not much concerned with the precise order of composition of the works which definitely belong to this group, but for interest I will add in brackets after each a number which denotes its position in Lutoslawski's 'presumed chronological order'. They are the *Apology* (1), the *Euthyphro* (2), the *Crito* (3), the *Charmides* (4), the *Laches* (5), the *Euthydemus* (8), the *Hippias major* (omitted by Lutoslawski as 'of dubious authenticity') and the *Hippias minor*, *Ion*, and *Lysis* (all three of which Lutoslawski also omits as 'of no logical importance': *Origin and Growth of Plato's Logic*, p. 75 n.). The three more controversial dialogues are the *Protagoras* (6), the *Meno* (7), the *Gorgias* (9) [*op. cit.* pp. 162–8].

The works that are definitely regarded as early have, with the exception of the *Apology* which stands by itself, certain marked characteristics in common, none of which are to be found in the late group of dialogues, while all, or almost all, are obtrusively prominent in, for instance, the *Laches*. First and most obvious, Socrates is always at this stage the central figure. Invariably, with his well-known irony and professions of ignorance, he sets about the merciless exposure of the self-satisfied blindness of the alleged expert, the politician, the general, the priest or the poet. There is constant reference to the craftsman, who, knowing what he wants to do or make, and how to set about his task in accordance with a clearly preconceived plan, provides an example of the kind of knowledge which the alleged expert should but does not possess. Socrates is constantly represented as doing what Aristotle in the *Metaphysics* tells us that he did, namely using inductive arguments in the search for universal definitions. Yet those definitions are never forthcoming. The positive conclusions which emerge from these lively little dialogues are very few and to be read mainly between the lines. The individual virtues, such as courage, self-discipline or piety, cannot be defined in isolation; all virtue is one and indissoluble; such virtue is a form of knowledge, knowledge of what is right and wrong; this particular form of knowledge, however, cannot be taught, it can only be discovered for oneself from one's own inner experience; once discovered it automatically brings happiness with it, as it did to Socrates himself; and so all wrong-doing is involuntary, arising from ignorance and resulting in damage to oneself. These are the doctrines briefly but eloquently expanded in chapter II of Cornford's little book *Before and After Socrates*. With Cornford, I find it irresistible to ascribe them to Socrates himself and to suppose that these early dialogues were written as soon as they could be after Socrates' death as Plato's memorial to his beloved friend. Whether they were written in Athens itself, in Megara, or indeed anywhere else, matters little. The important question is whether or not they were written as a group, in a relatively short time, at the stage in Plato's career described in the excerpt already quoted from *Epistle* VII as follows: 'The result was that I, who had

at first been full of eagerness to take part in public affairs
... eventually felt quite giddy. I did not cease to consider
in what possible way all these things might be improved
... but all the time I was waiting for the right moment for
action.' I believe that they were. I believe that Plato, dis-
illusioned with politics and politicians, bitterly hurt and
angered by the judicial murder of Socrates, decided at this
stage in his life that the only useful thing he could do in
the present circumstances was to paint a series of minia-
tures which would at once perpetuate the memory of his
friend and reveal by what manner of men he had been
put to death.

Here, however, we meet another formidable hurdle.
A number of distinguished scholars, Burnet, Taylor and
Shorey among them, have argued forcibly that already
in these early dialogues there are passages in which the
doctrine of Ideas or Forms is not only implied but explicitly propounded; and if that is the case, once again the
whole thesis of this book collapses. In brief, the doctrine
of Ideas, the development of which I shall attempt to trace
in detail later on, amounts to this: that underlying the
diversity of the sensible and mutable particulars of this
world, the objects that surround us and the actions in
which we are involved, there is another world of realities,
insensible and immutable, which are called the Ideas or
Forms, and from which the sensible world and its contents derive whatever degree of reality they possess.
Such, in barest outline, is the doctrine the presence or
absence of which in the early dialogues is a truly crucial
question in the histories both of Socrates and of Plato.

There is a passage in the *Euthyphro*, according to Luto-slawski the earliest actual dialogue of the whole series, which I think all scholars would agree presents the problem in the clearest possible colours. It begins at 6d9 and runs literally as follows:

SOCRATES: Remember then that you are not doing what I asked. I didn't ask you to teach me one or two of the many instances of piety, but rather that essential form by which all pious things are pious; for you said that it was by one common form that impious things are impious and pious things pious; or don't you remember?

EUTHYPHRO: Yes, I do.

SOCRATES: Then teach me the nature of this essential form so that by gazing at it and using it as my model, I may call any of your actions, or anybody else's, which has this character pious, but not so whatever has not got this character.

Shorey is fully justified in writing of this passage (*What Plato Said*, p. 75): 'The language of the definition here is undistinguishable from the language of the metaphysical theory of ideas in "later" dialogues.' The two different but cognate Greek words which I have been reduced to rendering alike by the English word 'form' are the two most regular of Plato's words for an Idea; indeed one of them is precisely that word in Greek letters and has naturally enough given rise to one of the two normal English names for the doctrine. And the metaphor of a model at which the philosopher gazes to the exclusion of all else persists into the third and last group of Plato's writings. Those scholars, however, who deduce from this undisputed fact (as well, of course, as from other much more disputable considerations) that the whole theory of Ideas must have been well known not only to Socrates himself but to his Pythagorean predecessors can do so only by ignoring or underestimating the most important and authoritative of all our scraps of ancient evidence on this particular question. At *Metaphysics* M 1078 b 30 Aristotle writes in so many words: 'But whereas Socrates did not regard his universals as separable nor his definitions, they [i.e. Plato and his followers] attributed separate existence to them and gave to this class of realities the name of Ideas.' This passage, which follows almost immediately upon that to which I referred earlier to the effect that Socrates' two contributions to the history of philosophy were inductive reasoning and general definition, contains, just like the earlier sentence, a straightforward statement of fact. No use, therefore, to argue in this instance, as we fairly can in many other contexts, that Aristotle's criticism of his predecessors' views is invalidated by his avowed object of seeing what anticipations he can find in earlier thinkers of his own doctrines. Here we have, as I say, a bald statement of fact, not a prejudiced criticism. It is a fact, moreover, which Aristotle, if anybody, had every opportunity of knowing. For the best part of twenty years he was Plato's pupil in the Academy. It is inconceivable that during that time Plato's relations with Socrates should not have been often discussed or that Aristotle should have been wrong when he wrote these brief but vital sentences.

But in that case some other explanation must be given of Shorey's unassailable statement that the language of the

Euthyphro 'is undistinguishable from the language of the metaphysical theory of ideas in "later" dialogues'. Such an explanation is not hard to find; it has been given by various scholars in various forms often enough before. What Socrates is asking Euthyphro to do is to stop pointing to individual acts of piety and to tell him instead the common characteristic of all pious acts by reference to which he may know that he is justified in calling one particular act pious, another impious. Suppose that for simplicity's sake, we substitute for pious acts something more palpably concrete such as pigs. Such a substitution is quite legitimate for two reasons: first because the pious actions with which Socrates was concerned were, just like pigs, a part of the world of sensible experience; and second because to the mature Plato there was evidently an Idea of Pig, and of every other natural species, just as much as there was an Idea of Piety, and of every other virtue. Then the passage becomes perfectly simple and straightforward. 'I am not asking you', says Socrates, 'to show me one or two pigs but rather to describe to me the essential form of a pig by which a pig is a pig; the common characteristics of all pigs, by reference to which I may be enabled, whenever I see a pig, to recognize it as a pig, a whole pig and nothing but a pig.' And that is something wholly different from maintaining, as Plato would have maintained by the time he wrote the *Republic* and the *Phaedrus*, that we recognize a pig when we see it because, in a celestial pre-natal existence, we were privileged to gaze on the Idea of Pig itself. That is what is involved in Aristotle's typically dry remark that the

Platonists gave a separate existence to their universals and called them Ideas. It is surely quite easy to suppose that Socrates already used a vocabulary to some words of which Plato considerably later came to attach a more profound significance than Socrates himself had ever contemplated.

To sum up an already summary discussion of a thorny topic, there are ultimately two extreme views on the subject between which, so far as I can see, no compromise is logically defensible. There is either the evolutionary theory, that Plato's metaphysical doctrines first grew out of Socrates' search in the ethical field for universal definitions, and went on growing for the rest of his long life; or there is the static theory, that Plato had already arrived at all his most fundamental beliefs before he ever put pen to paper and deliberately withheld what he regarded as the very kernel of the truth, the theory of Ideas as it is developed in the *Republic*, until he had written the *Apology* and at least a dozen dialogues which tell his readers nothing about it but which are solely devoted to that out of which the theory grew. The latter view, though it has been seriously held, strikes me as too fantastic to merit any consideration. Of course an artist such as Plato, if there ever were just such another, could well have carried a theory in his head for years before he found occasion to mention it in a dialogue. But, with that necessary proviso, I believe that, when we can actually watch, as I hope to show that we can, the theory of Ideas taking shape and growing like an embryo in Plato's own writings, it is perverse to reject, though not necessarily perverse to modify, the evolutionary theory.

CHAPTER 4

'PROTAGORAS' AND 'GORGIAS'

The question of the relative dates of the *Protagoras*, the *Gorgias* and the *Meno* is one which has always exercised Plato's readers and, as usual, opinions differ sharply and widely. Lutoslawski, from his mainly stylometric standpoint, thought the *Protagoras* the sixth of Plato's works, the *Meno*, to be discussed in detail in the next chapter, the seventh and the *Gorgias* the ninth. Taylor (*op. cit.* p. 103) writes of the *Gorgias*: 'As we shall see when we come to deal with the *Protagoras*, the ethical doctrine of the dialogues is identical, and it is inconceivable to me that any reader of literary sensibility can doubt which of the two is the product of a riper mastery of dramatic art'; of the *Meno* he says (*ibid.* p. 130) that 'there ought to be no doubt that the *Meno* is a cruder and earlier work than either of the two great dramatic dialogues with which it is most intimately connected, the *Phaedo* and the *Protagoras*'; and he treats the *Protagoras* itself as one of the middle group of dialogues and discusses it after the *Phaedo* and the *Symposium* and immediately before the *Republic*. In his recent edition of the *Gorgias* Professor Dodds writes (pp. 21–2): 'Artistically too, as well as philosophically, the *Protagoras* appears much less mature: I think the majority of unprejudiced readers will agree with Friedländer (II², 324) that the *Gorgias* is "incomparably deeper and more intense", as well as better constructed'; a page later he writes: 'The *Meno* is closely linked with the *Gorgias* by its references to the great Athenian statesmen of the fifth century, to Gorgias himself, and to the Pythagorean σοφοί: hence there is now general agreement that the two are close together in date. But the order of composition is disputed'; and he adds a a little later that 'the arguments for the priority of the *Gorgias* are the stronger'. Those three opinions out of many which might be cited must suffice to illustrate the extent of the divergence. Although I thereby incur Taylor's charge of literary insensibility, I wholeheartedly subscribe so far to the views of Dodds.

Even Taylor, whose verdict on this particular question is for many invalidated by his belief that Socrates had held the Platonic theory of Ideas, admits in the introduction to his chapter on the *Protagoras* that 'the central purpose of the dialogue is to exhibit clearly the ultimate ethical presuppositions of the Socratic morality and the "sophistic" morality at its best, and to show exactly where they are in irreconcilable opposition'; and in the brief 'general analysis' which precedes this sentence he includes both the 'Socratic "paradox" of the unity of the virtues' and 'the further developments that the one thing to which all forms of "goodness" reduce is seen to be "knowledge", and the consequence . . . that "all wrongdoing is error"'. The *Protagoras* is in fact, in almost every respect, a thoroughly Socratic dialogue. Admittedly it is planned on a larger scale and it may be more dramatically vivid than most of the early works; but even the *Apology* can hardly be said to lack dramatic artistry, and I should myself hesitate to distinguish on this account between, say, the *Laches* and the *Protagoras*. Otherwise, it seems to be a typical addition to the early group. Although Protagoras is sympathetically portrayed and allowed, despite some protest, to discourse at length, Socrates once again controls the course of the conversation; there is the familiar irony and satire, at the expense of Prodicus and Hippias, and indeed the Sophists in general, as well as of Protagoras; there is no mention or even premonition of the theory of Ideas; and the dialogue ends, like the rest of the early group, in ostensible failure to solve the problem under discussion, which task, says Socrates, is impossible until we have first established the nature of virtue itself. Indeed, as he goes on to point out, he and Protagoras have by the end of the conversation exchanged the positions from which each started. Whereas at the outset Protagoras claimed not only that virtue could be taught but also to teach it himself, while Socrates began by maintaining that it was unteachable, by the end Protagoras is disputing Socrates' thesis that, since all virtue is knowledge, it must be possible to teach or learn it.

In common with many other of Plato's dialogues, particularly the early ones, the *Protagoras* contains a good deal of quibbling and even of false logic; at times Plato himself was clearly aware of the fact. But there is one particular stage in the conversation which has given rise to prolonged debate as to whether or not Plato could possibly have been in earnest. The vexed passage begins at 351 b 3 and runs as follows:

Do you say, Protagoras, said I, that some men live well, others ill?

Yes, he said.

Then do you think that a man would be living well if he lived in vexation and pain?

No.

What then if he lived in pleasure to the end of his life? Don't you think that he would have lived well?

Yes, I do.

In that case to live in pleasure is a good thing, to live without pleasure a bad.

Yes, if a man lives in pleasure of honourable things.

What, Protagoras? Surely you too don't, like the masses, call some pleasures bad and some pains good? I mean, in so far as they are pleasant, aren't they to that extent good, provided that nothing different results from them? And again, isn't just the same true with pains? In so far as they are painful, aren't they evil?

I don't know that I should answer that question, Socrates, in quite the simple terms in which you put it, that all pleasures are good and all pains evil.

This passage, which I have rendered as literally and accurately as I can, very largely explains the ultimate exchange by the protagonists of their original positions. At first sight it may appear to reveal an astounding reversal of all that Socrates, or for that matter Plato, normally stood for. At the same time it is conceived and written with so subtle an irony that it is by no means only Protagoras and the other Sophists present who have fallen into the trap. Socrates, say countless critics, some apologetically, some in bewilderment and some in triumph, suddenly appears as the champion of out-and-out Hedonism, equating the good with the pleasant and urging that the whole of human life be guided by constant reference to a scale of pleasures and pains. At what stage in his life, they ask, and for what conceivable motive, can Plato have seen fit to represent his master as holding the very creed which, in many other dialogues, most notably the *Gorgias*, he is portrayed as vehemently attacking? Nowhere else in the whole of Plato's writings is there the slightest suggestion that Socrates had ever regarded the equation of good with pleasure with anything but abhorrence.

This fantastic problem, which has tended to obscure the issue of the date of composition of the *Protagoras*, seems to me to rest on a total misconception. I realize that I am here in conflict with much of the most weighty authority. Dodds for example has recently written (*op. cit.* p. 21 n. 3):

Scholars who resent the suggestion that Plato ever changed his mind have tried to paper over this crack in the 'unity' of his thought by methods which seem to me more ingenious than intellectually honest. The dialogue contains no hint that the assumption is made merely for the sake of argument—and why should it be, since it is *not* the assumption of Protagoras (351 d), or even of 'the many' (352 d e)?

But I do not think it involves much ingenuity or any intellectual dishonesty to make the following three points, which between them should remove the difficulty.

First, and least important, even my brief summary in the last chapter of those beliefs which may reasonably be attributed to Socrates contained the belief that happiness automatically springs from goodness, from following the dictates of conscience. There is, so far as I can see, no suggestion in this passage of the *Protagoras* (which anyhow is based entirely, as Adam pointed out in his edition of the dialogue (p. xxix), on the fallacy of assuming without argument the equation of 'well' with 'pleasantly') as to what is the nature of the pleasure which Socrates is said to be advocating. It is true that later on (353 c6) Socrates mentions 'food and drink and love' as 'pleasant things', but he immediately adds that 'though you know them to be evil, you still indulge in them'. Is there any firm ground, especially in a dialogue as admittedly satirical as the *Protagoras*, for the widespread conviction that the Hedonism which Socrates is said to be preaching is Hedonism in the normal sense of the word?

And if, as it may be, this argument is dismissed as a mere quibble, then there is a second argument which I believe to be very much stronger. There is no firm ground, either, for the repeated assertion that, in the crucial passage quoted above, Socrates is made to put forward Hedonism as his own creed. I strongly suspect that that assertion often rests on a mistranslation of a single phrase. In the penultimate speech of the excerpt, the middle sentence is rendered by Jowett, for instance: 'for I am rather disposed to say that things are good in as far as they are pleasant, if they have no consequences of another sort'.[1] That is not what the sentence means, if only because what Plato wrote is incontrovertibly a question, not an expression of opinion. I am sure that my own rendering, which replaces the misleading 'I am rather disposed to say' with 'I mean . . .', gives the true sense. As Adam writes in his

[1] ἐγὼ γὰρ λέγω, καθ' ὃ ἡδέα ἐστίν, ἆρα κατὰ τοῦτο οὐκ ἀγαθά;

note on the passage: 'Socrates puts his question in a different form inviting an affirmative answer.' The crucial sentences which introduce the new stage in the conversation are in fact all in the form 'Do you say, Protagoras, . . .?', 'Do you think . . .?' or 'Don't you think . . .?'[1] It is neither necessary nor justifiable to say that Socrates suddenly appears as the champion of Hedonism. This time I follow Taylor (*op. cit.* p. 260) against Dodds in maintaining that 'neither Protagoras nor Socrates is represented as adopting the Hedonist equation of good with pleasure. The thesis which Socrates is committed to is simply that of the identity of goodness and knowledge.' And when Taylor continues, as he does at once, that 'the further identification of good with pleasure is carefully treated . . . as one neither to be affirmed nor denied', I would again agree; but with the addition that Plato's motives may well have been rather more malicious than Taylor's sentence suggests. Throughout the whole dialogue, and especially here, Plato seems to me to be deriving the utmost amusement from the attempt to manœuvre the distinguished Sophist into the very position which he began by repudiating. His tactics are not always fair, but they are always, in one sense or another, *ad hominem*.

So, finally, to Dodds' contention that 'the dialogue contains no hint that the assumption is made merely for the sake of argument—and why should it be, since it is *not* the assumption of Protagoras, or even the many?' That may be true of the *Protagoras* itself, where Protagoras is, as

[1] λέγεις. . ., ὦ Πρωταγόρα, . . .;, ἆρ οὖν δοκεῖ σοι. . .;, οὐκ. . .σοι δοκεῖ. . .;

I have said, sympathetically portrayed. But Plato's real enemy at this stage was not Protagoras, nor Gorgias, nor any other individual sophist, but the morality which he believed that the whole sophistic movement had consciously or unconsciously inculcated. And that morality, as many a passage from Plato shows, was based on the belief that might is right and that the object of the strong is, and should be, to secure for themselves a maximum of pleasure. The *Protagoras* is a particularly subtle part of Plato's campaign against the sophistic morality; so subtle indeed that it has caused a great deal more confusion than he can have anticipated when he wrote it. Taylor was probably justified, though he pushed the point much too far, when he took this subtlety, and the dramatic artistry which accompanies it, as proof of a relatively late date of composition. In all essentials the *Protagoras* looks not only like one of the latest of the early group, but also like a brilliantly conceived and brilliantly executed preparation for the dialogue which I believe must follow closely after it, the *Gorgias*.

The primary purpose of the *Gorgias*, unlike that of the *Protagoras*, is immediately obvious and, so far as I know, has never been disputed. The two irreconcilable ideals of life, the Socratic and the sophistic, around which Plato flits almost playfully in other dialogues, are here brought into direct and deadly conflict. In consequence Socrates is here for once, in contrast to all the dialogues of the early group, allowed to abandon his usual role of ironic enquirer and to put forward his own point of view with passionate conviction. This time not only his opponents, Gorgias himself, Polus and Callicles, but Socrates too, though apologetically, are all allowed to indulge in what Socrates normally deplores, long speeches. The *Gorgias* is therefore, in its presentation if not in its content, sharply distinguished from all the dialogues of the early group.

Another curious point about the *Gorgias* is that, again in contrast to most of Plato's dialogues, the date at which the discussion is supposed to have taken place is impossible to fix. As Dodds says (*op. cit.* p. 17):

In what year are we to imagine the conversation as taking place? If Plato ever asked himself this question (which may perhaps be doubted), his answer must have been, 'In no particular year'. For, as Herodicus of Babylon already noticed . . ., no ingenuity can reconcile the various chronological data which he has obligingly supplied.

That fact calls for explanation.

Any reader of the *Gorgias*, whatever his literary sensibility, can hardly fail to detect in it a tone of vehemence, almost of bitterness, which is to be heard in very few other passages of Plato's writings. In a speech of remarkable power Callicles, the young candidate for political office, who, like Plato himself, commands wealth and social influence but unlike Plato has no scruples to hold him back, contrasts the active life of the politician, which is alone worthy of the naturally strong and free, with the retired life of the philosopher, who knows nothing of the world and its ways or of the pleasures, desires and ambitions of ordinary men. Philosophy may be all very well for the young, but nothing could be more contemptible than the sight of an older man 'creeping away to spend the rest of his life whispering with three or four striplings in a corner' (485 d 6). And now at last Socrates turns and rends his adversary, the practising politician; he denounces the political egoist as the enemy of society; he formulates his own contrasting ideal of a virtue which implies the inward harmony of perfect self-mastery; and he finally claims (521 d 6): 'I think I am one of few Athenians, not to say the only one, who attempts the true art of statesmanship, the only man alive who really does the business of the state.'

The choice between philosophy and politics as a way of life is not one that can ever have disturbed the real Socrates. The bitterness of the *Gorgias* points in exactly the same direction as the other indications that I have already mentioned. Plato is thinking of his own situation, of the choice which he himself has to make. The *Gorgias* contains his final answer to the overtures of his political friends and relations, the answer that true statesmanship cannot exist unless hand in hand with true philosophy. In the words of the excerpt from *Epistle* VII quoted in the last chapter:

In the end I saw clearly that, in the case of all existing states, their government is without exception bad. Their systems are virtually incurable without a combination of inspired planning and good fortune. I was forced to assert, in praise of genuine philosophy, that only from that standpoint was it possible to get a true view of public and private right, and that accordingly the human race would never have respite from its troubles until either the true and genuine philosophers gain political control or else those who are already governing in the states become, by some divine dispensation, real philosophers.

It was with this conviction that I first went to Italy and Sicily . . .

The theoretical or ideal solution indicated in these sentences is not, of course, worked out in detail until the *Republic*, which, however, may well have been already beginning to take shape at the back of Plato's mind. For Plato himself, in the actual world in which he lived, no perfect solution was available. But meanwhile, the *Gorgias* seems to me, as it has seemed to many others, to contain Plato's reluctant farewell to the political life of his own city, Athens. As the passage already quoted from *Epistle* VII suggests, the *Gorgias* was probably written shortly before Plato left Athens for his first visit to Italy and Sicily.

Here, however, we once again run into a difficulty. *Epistle* VII continues, from the point at which we left it:

But when I arrived, the kind of life that is there called happy, sated with Italian and Syracusan feasts, a life consisting of stuffing oneself full twice a day, never going to sleep alone at night, and all the usual practices associated with such an existence, filled me with utter disgust. No man under heaven, brought up from youth in such habits, could ever become wise —so miraculous a character is incompatible with such a life— nor would he have any prospect of acquiring self-control; and the same would be true of all other forms of goodness. No state, moreover, could ever be at peace with itself, under any laws of whatever kind, so long as its citizens thought it right to spend everything on excesses and to undertake no activity whatever except banquets and drinking parties and whole-hearted devotion to sex. It is inevitable that such states should become tyrannies, oligarchies, democracies in a ceaseless succession, while the very mention of just and equal government is intolerable to those in control.

With this added to my earlier beliefs I travelled on to Syracuse.

Now surely, a number of scholars have said, believing as I do in the historical reliability if not necessarily in the Platonic authorship of *Epistle* VII, this passage suggests that the *Gorgias* must have been written shortly after rather than shortly before Plato's first visit to the West. It must have been his disgust at the excesses of the Italians and Sicilians that induced Plato to write a dialogue in which the opposed ideals of life are eventually brought face to face in open conflict and in which his own notion of true statesmanship is at last explicitly revealed. And several other indications point the same way. Already in the *Gorgias* there are traces of a new and significant interest in Pythagoreanism, which Plato can most naturally be supposed to have acquired in the West; I shall be discussing these traces in a little more detail in the next chapter. There is the well-known passage beginning at 493 a 1, which has been supposed to refer to the Pythagorean Philolaus, in which Socrates says:

I once heard one of the sages say that we are now dead, that the body is a tomb and that the part of the soul in which our desires arise is liable to over-persuasion and vacillation to and fro; and so some smart chap, perhaps a Sicilian or an Italian, made up an allegory in which, by a play on words, he called this part, as being so pliable and persuasible, a jar, while the unwise he called uninitiated.[1]

And more significant still, there is the reference at 518b6 to 'Mithaecus, the author of the Sicilian cookery-book'. These considerations, and several others of less weight, all go to show that the *Gorgias* should be dated after the Sicilian visit.

This argument has some force, but it is by no means conclusive. I do not intend to discuss the question in detail since, compared with the problem of the relative dates of the three dialogues, *Protagoras*, *Gorgias* and *Meno*, it is of minor importance. My own opinion is based upon a single argument which is frankly subjective and would be rejected by Shorey and his followers. Both psychologically and on the evidence of *Epistle* VII it seems to me more natural to suppose that Plato had already reached and published his decision to renounce the politics of Athens before he left for the West. He must have begun, very soon after his return from Sicily, on the elaboration of his own as opposed to Socrates' philosophy. The *Gorgias*, to my mind, marks the culmination of the essentially Socratic phase of his life, while the *Meno* marks the beginning of a new and more creative phase. It is difficult to imagine Plato on his return to Athens, when he must have been pregnant with new thoughts, finding time to write a dialogue which, however many allusions it may

[1] I can think of no natural rendering that would reproduce either the 'play on words' between πιθανόν and πίθον or the fanciful derivation of ἀμυήτους.

contain to Sicily (which was, after all, Gorgias' own home-country), contains also essentially, though now more positively, the same teaching as the rest of the early group and only the very faintest, if any, premonitions of the teaching of the group which is to follow. But the question will probably always remain a matter of opinion.

Although it is not strictly relevant to my main purpose to follow *Epistle* VII any further, one more brief excerpt must be quoted from it purely for its intrinsic interest. The passage begins at 327a1, a mere seven lines after the end of the last excerpt:

In my dealings with Dion, who was then a young man, I disclosed to him my theoretical ideas for mankind and urged him to put them into practice; and I am afraid that I did not realize that, quite unconsciously, I was in a sense devising the overthrow of tyranny. Anyhow Dion, who was generally quick to learn, and especially so with the arguments I put to him on this occasion, responded more keenly and wholeheartedly than any young man I have ever met. He chose to live the rest of his life quite differently from the majority of Italians and Sicilians, cherishing virtue more dearly than pleasure or luxury in general. For this reason his way of life, till the time of Dionysius' death, was far from popular with those who live in accordance with the fashions of tyrants.

Such is Plato's (or pseudo-Plato's) account of the beginning of his first practical attempt to produce a philosopher-king. This first attempt was doomed to failure. The second attempt, the foundation of the Academy as a training-ground for future statesmen, was to have more effective and enduring results.

CHAPTER 5

'MENO'

Although the last chapter should have made my opinion on the approximate date of the *Gorgias* clear enough, one further question must be discussed before I move on to the *Meno*. Some scholars have contrived to see in the *Gorgias*, alongside the new interest in Pythagoreanism, a clear premonition of the yet newer theory of Ideas. The interest in Pythagoreanism is found not only in the passage quoted in the last chapter, but chiefly also in the reference in 507e–508a to the 'wise men' who 'tell us that heaven and earth, gods and men are held together by communion and friendship, orderliness, self-control and justice, and that this is the reason why this whole world is called by the name of order (Cosmos), not disorder'; in the allusion, which follows almost immediately, to 'geometrical equality'; in certain features of the myth which virtually rounds the whole dialogue off, notably the inclusion of the doctrine of a Purgatory which, as Dodds says (*op. cit.* p. 375) 'prepared its victims not for Heaven but for a return to Earth'; and in the use on at least four occasions of mathematical illustrations. The foreshadowing of the theory of Ideas is said to be discernible not only in the occasional use of words and metaphors which were later a regular part of the vocabulary of the theory, but especially in a sentence at 503d–e which runs as follows:

The good man, who speaks with the best intention, will surely say what he says not at random, but with his eyes fixed on something; just like all other craftsmen, each of whom brings what he does bring to his own work, not from random selection, but with a view to achieving a certain form in what he is making.

While there are perhaps more traces of Pythagorean influence in the *Gorgias* than in any dialogue that precedes it, these traces hardly strengthen the view that Plato must have visited the Pythagoreans in the West before the *Gorgias* was written. Despite the Pythagoreans' well-known oath of secrecy, Plato could and would have learnt, whether at first hand from Pythagoreans who came to Greece proper or only at second hand, at least as much about Pythagorean doctrine as is contained in the *Gorgias*. There are far more striking signs of Pythagorean influence in the *Meno* than there are in the *Gorgias*; but that is by no means the strongest reason for electing to date the *Meno* the later of the two. And as for the contention that the passage just quoted foreshadows the theory of Ideas, this particular passage does not seem to do so nearly as plainly as the passage from the *Euthyphro* already quoted and discussed in chapter 3. For the moment, therefore, we will accept, as Dodds does, the verdict of Lutoslawski (*The Origin and Growth of Plato's Logic*, p. 217) that 'here we have only the germ from which the theory of ideas was afterwards developed'. Our primary concern at this stage is whether the *Gorgias* was written before or after the *Meno*.

In three separate respects the *Meno* differs from any

dialogue so far discussed: it differs in form, it differs in method and it differs in content.

As regards the form, there is little to be said and that little is scarcely controversial. To show that I am not over-simplifying, I shall give R. S. Bluck's analysis of the argument of the *Meno* in his recent edition (p. 4) rather than my own.

The *Meno* may be divided into the following sections:

1. The question 'Is virtue teachable?' raises the prior question 'What is virtue?' Attempts are made to define virtue. Meno is reduced to ἀπορία (80a).

2. The question 'How can you look for something you don't know, or recognize it if you find it?' causes Socrates to propound the theory that the soul is immortal, and that learning is recollection of knowledge acquired before birth. Socrates illustrates the theory by questioning one of Meno's slaves (80d–85b).

3. Meno again asks, 'Is virtue teachable?' Socrates undertakes to investigate the question ... by means of a hypothesis, a method used by geometricians:

Let us suppose that virtue is a kind of knowledge. If it is, it will be teachable; otherwise it will not (87e).

But virtue is knowledge (88d, 89a).

Therefore virtue is teachable (89c).

4. Socrates suggests that there is an objection to this conclusion. If a thing is teachable, there ought to be teachers of it (89d–e). But there are no teachers of virtue (96b). Therefore virtue cannot be teachable after all (96c).

5. Virtue is not knowledge but 'true belief'. It is not teachable and comes θείᾳ μοίρᾳ ἄνευ νοῦ—unless some statesman should be found who is capable of making a statesman of another (96e–100b).

Epilogue (100b): we can only be certain of the right answer if, before asking how virtue comes, we try to discover what its essential nature is.

This analysis has been quoted in full as an excellent introduction to every point in the *Meno* that I wish to discuss. For the moment, however, we are concerned only with its first two paragraphs.

Paragraph 1 might well be imagined to be an exceptionally brief résumé of a typical minor dialogue of the early group. The question which it raises is a familiar Socratic question; for the first ten or so pages (by the traditional numbering the *Meno* begins at 70a) the discussion follows the familiar Socratic pattern; and this first section concludes with Socrates' interlocutor reduced to the familiar ἀπορία or impasse. Meno likens Socrates to an Electric Ray Fish, which benumbs anybody who touches it, and at this stage a typical early dialogue would have ended. Not so the *Meno*. In the *Meno*, as the second paragraph of Bluck's analysis shows, it is only at this stage that Plato, by raising an entirely unfamiliar problem, begins on his serious business. We must not build too much on the novelty of the *Meno*'s form; but when that novelty coincides, as it does, with a novelty of both method and content it surely has some significance.

The new method is very briefly summarized in Bluck's third paragraph: 'Socrates undertakes to investigate the question . . . by means of a hypothesis, a method used by geometricians.' Here is a fuller, but still not quite a full, rendering of the passage in question, which begins at 86e2:

SOCRATES: ... Do consent to investigate the question whether virtue is teachable, or how else it is acquired, on a hypothesis. By 'on a hypothesis' I mean this: just as geometricians, when somebody asks them, for instance, if a given area could be inscribed as a triangle in a particular circle, often consider the question and might reply: 'I don't yet know whether it's possible, but I think it may help to solve the problem to make a sort of hypothesis such as this: if the area is of such and such a nature ... [and here follow some barely intelligible geometrical details], then one thing seems to follow, whereas if it is not such, then something different follows. So I would like to make a hypothesis and then tell you how its consequences affect the possibility of inscribing the area in the circle.' In the same way let us make a hypothesis concerning virtue, since we don't know what it is or of what kind, and investigate the question whether it is teachable or not in the following terms: to what class of things concerned with the soul must virtue belong if it is to be teachable or unteachable? First of all, if virtue is different from knowledge, is it or is it not teachable? Or, as we were saying just now, can it be recollected? It shouldn't matter which term we use. But is it teachable? Surely this much is clear to everyone, that a man can be taught nothing but knowledge?

MENO: It seems so to me.

SOCRATES: So if virtue is a kind of knowledge, it's clear that it must be teachable.

MENO: Surely.

SOCRATES: That's quickly over then; if virtue is of this nature, then it's teachable, and otherwise it isn't.

MENO: Yes, certainly.

Unfortunately, this passage leads us back at once on to difficult and dangerous ground, which, since it lies only on the margin of our subject, must be traversed rapidly.

The problems raised in the passage are discussed in detail in Richard Robinson's book, *Plato's Earlier Dialectic*, and again by Bluck in the section of his introduction entitled 'The Hypothetical Method' (*op. cit.* pp. 75–108). By no means only the geometrical details in Socrates' speech are obscure; scholars are not yet agreed on at least three questions of much greater importance. First, exactly what is the method of the geometricians which Socrates professes to borrow? Is it or is it not geometrical analysis? Second, exactly what hypothesis does Socrates himself proceed to make in the sequel to this passage? Is it, as seems superficially self-evident, the simple hypothesis that virtue is knowledge or is it something more complex? And third, how much value anyway does Plato attach to the method, since the proposition which it is used to establish, namely that virtue, being knowledge, must be teachable, is promptly demolished again? A detailed discussion of such questions would take too long and, important though they are, I shall leave them largely unanswered, concentrating rather on the only two points which immediately concern us.

In the first place, I am sure, although the point has been disputed, that Plato himself believes that he is introducing a new method. Otherwise, what can be the object of the relatively long digression to explain the meaning of the word 'on a hypothesis'? As in the *Gorgias*, so again here, we note Plato's significant interest in mathematics; but here for the first time he is explicitly concerned with the method which mathematicians use. An earlier passage of the *Meno*, that in which Socrates illustrates the theory that all learning is recollection by inducing a slave-boy, by a series of leading questions, to 'recollect' that the square on the diameter of another square is twice as large as that other square, has already pointed the same way. Plato is, in the *Meno*, beginning to reveal a new interest in mathematics as in some way directly relevant to other fields of enquiry. And when, in the passage quoted earlier, he suddenly borrows the mathematicians' method of employing a positive proposition in an attempt to prove, rather than disprove, something else, he seems once again to be taking a significant step forward.

In the second place, nobody who has read the *Phaedo*, which by common consent must have been written not very long after the *Meno*, could deny that by that stage in Plato's life the hypothetical method, so briefly and confusingly introduced in the *Meno* passage, has already for Plato assumed a central position. The relevant passage from the *Phaedo* will be discussed in the next chapter. Those scholars strike me as over-cautious and perverse who reject as invalid or even illegitimate the kind of argument I am now using. Plato seems to have demonstrably developed and clarified his method between finishing the *Meno* and starting on the *Phaedo*. As Robinson says at the end of his chapter on 'Hypothesis in the *Meno*' (*op. cit.* p. 122),

The *Meno's* discussion of hypothetical method seems to have value as the symbol of a valuable change in Plato's writings. With the introduction of this method he is passing from destructive to constructive thinking, from elenchus and the refutation of other men's views to the elaboration of positive views of his own. The dialogue begins with refutations of Meno's definitions of virtue, and ends with attempts to say something positive about virtue, even if tentative and non-essential, by means of the hypothetical method. It is thus a microcosm of the whole series of Plato's dialogues; for on the whole those previous to the *Meno* are merely destructive and those after it are definitely constructive.

Had Robinson not written it first, that is exactly what I should have wished to say myself.

And what seems clear enough about the method of the *Meno* seems even clearer about the third and last and most interesting aspect of the *Meno's* novelty, its new doctrine. Here there are are two separate but closely related passages of particular importance, the first of which, as Bluck's summary shows, comes some pages before the excerpt which we have just been considering concerning the new method. It begins at 81 a 5 and runs as follows:

SOCRATES: ... I have heard what men and women who are
    wise about matters divine have to say.
MENO: And what do they say?
SOCRATES: What seems to me true as well as beautiful.
MENO: What was it they said, and who were they anyhow?
SOCRATES: They were certain priests and priestesses who had
    taken pains to be able to give an account of their concerns;
    and Pindar says the same too, and many other poets of the
    inspired kind. This is what they tell us, and you should
    consider whether you think they are telling the truth.
    They say that the soul of man is immortal, that at one time
    it ceases—that is what is called death—and at another begins
    again, but that it is never destroyed. So we must live our
    whole lives through in all piety. For [and here follows a

fragment of verse, almost certainly from Pindar] 'from whomsoever Persephone accepts requital for grief of long ago, in the ninth year she restores their souls to the sunlight above. From them arise noble kings, and men of swift strength, and those who excel in wisdom. And for the rest of time they are called by mankind holy heroes.' So the soul, being immortal and born many times before, has already seen the things on earth and the things in Hades— indeed all things—and there is nothing that it has not already learnt. No wonder then that, in the case of virtue as in other cases, it is possible for the soul to recollect what it once knew. For all nature is akin, and since the soul has already learnt everything, there is nothing to prevent a man who has only recollected one single thing—that is what is called learning—from rediscovering everything else for himself, provided only that he has the fortitude and doesn't weary of the search. So the searching and the learning is entirely a matter of recollection.

And very soon after this passage comes the demonstration on the slave-boy.

Although about half the dialogue intervenes between the two passages with which we are at present concerned, they are so closely linked that I shall quote a part of the second before I discuss either. The passage begins at 96d, where Socrates raises the question of the difference, if any, between right opinion and knowledge. In practical matters, he says, right opinion produces the same results as knowledge: a guide with a right opinion about the way to Larissa will take you there just as surely as one who actually knows the way. Why then, wonders Meno at 97d, is knowledge so much more valuable than right opinion? Plato continues as follows:

SOCRATES: Do you know why you are puzzled, or would you like me to tell you?

MENO: Yes, by all means do.

SOCRATES: It's because you haven't paid enough attention to the statues of Daedalus; perhaps there aren't any where you live.

MENO: Why do you say that?

SOCRATES: Because these statues of his, unless they are firmly fastened, run away and play truant, whereas when once they are fastened they stay where they are.

MENO: Well, what then?

SOCRATES: Possessing one of his works which is at large is not much use; it's like having a runaway slave who won't stay where he is. But when it has been fastened down, it's very valuable; for his works are extremely beautiful. And why, you ask, do I say that? With a view to right opinions. For right opinions, so long as they stay where they are, are a beautiful thing and produce all manner of good effects. But for much of the time they refuse to stay where they are; they keep on running away from our souls, so that they're not worth much to their possessor until he fastens them down by thinking out the reason why. And that, Meno my friend, as we agreed earlier, means recollection. When they are fastened down they become knowledge, and thus stable. And that is the reason why knowledge is more valuable than right opinion; it differs in being fastened down.

A reader who is unfamiliar with Plato's idiosyncrasies might easily suppose him to be hinting that each of these passages should be taken with a grain of salt: in the first the doctrine of the immortality and transmigration of the soul is ascribed to certain anonymous 'priests and priestesses'; in the second there is the fanciful analogy to the fabled statues of Daedalus. Any such supposition would be

almost the opposite of the truth. We shall see when we
come to the magnificent passage from the *Symposium*
which I shall be quoting in chapter 8 that Plato on other
occasions than this saw fit to attribute to another what he
himself passionately believed. In the *Symposium* the
priestess is admittedly given a name, but there is grave
doubt whether such a one ever actually existed, let alone
instructed Socrates. Likewise the use of analogy or allegory, as we shall see in the central books of the *Republic*, is
a device to which Plato frequently resorted when he
wished to set down something of the kernel of his thought.
As *Epistle* VII tells us, at a stage far beyond that to which
we have so far followed it (341), nothing would ever
have persuaded Plato to summarize in a sort of handbook,
as others seem to have done, his profoundest beliefs.

Two much more important questions arising from the
first of these passages are whether or not these anonymous 'priests and priestesses' were real people and, if so,
who they were. Good reasons can be adduced for the
conjecture that the answer to the first question is Yes and
to the second The Pythagoreans.[1] We are lucky enough
to possess contemporary and trustworthy evidence, in a
fragment of the itinerant philosopher-poet Xenophanes
(fr. 7 *ap.* Diogenes Laertius VIII, 36), that Pythagoras
himself already believed in the transmigration of souls;
and the Neoplatonic writer Porphyry, who wrote in the

[1] I cannot here enter into the vexed question of the relationship between the Pythagoreans and the Orphics, which anyhow does not affect
the argument of the remainder of this paragraph. On this subject see
E. R. Dodds, *The Greeks and the Irrational*, chapter V.

latter half of the third century A.D., tells us in his *Life of Pythagoras* (19) that, of the Pythagorean doctrines which 'became universally known', the first was 'that the soul is immortal', the second 'that it changes into other kinds of living things' and the fourth and last 'that all living things should be regarded as akin'. It is probably not an accident or coincidence that Plato should have included in the first excerpt from the *Meno* the sentence 'For all nature is akin'. That he should have ascribed a doctrine which we know dates back to Pythagoras himself to 'certain priests and priestesses' cannot conceivably be an accident. As his increasing interest in mathematical method also suggests, Plato is at this stage of his life becoming more and more intimately concerned with the Pythagorean philosophy.

Some scholars have held that the *Meno* contains the earliest explicit formulation of the theory of Ideas. That is not strictly true, for the simple reason that there is as yet no account whatever of the nature or status of the things to be recollected. But on the other hand there can be no possible doubt that this time the theory is not only foreshadowed but presupposed. We have to await the *Phaedo* for an explicit formulation of the theory, but in that respect the *Phaedo* is merely tackling a problem which the *Meno* has already raised. Again Plato seems to be working gradually forward. As Bluck says (*Plato's 'Meno'*, p. 110), 'it is natural to suppose that once Plato had turned his attention to these (for him) all-important matters in the *Meno*, no very long interval elapsed before the writing of the *Phaedo*'. Perhaps the chief interest and

67

importance of the *Meno* lie in the subsequent developments of the doctrines which the dialogue is the first to
adumbrate.

The same applies even more forcibly to the second
passage just quoted, where Plato tells us that right belief
can only be converted into knowledge by 'thinking out
the reason why'; and that is itself, he adds, the same as
recollection. We are given no details in the *Meno* of what
is involved in this process of 'thinking out the reason
why'; again we have to await later dialogues for a description, or as much of a description as we ever get, of
what it involves. But again the same strong impression
emerges that Plato has lately run on to a new line of
thought, which he will follow further as soon as he can.

So we reach the final questions arising from the *Meno*,
and they are the most significant because they focus all
that has been said so far on a single point. What has happened to Plato at this stage of his life to induce him to
abandon the Socratic elenchus in favour of constructive
teaching? What has led him to a new interest in mathematical method? Why has he suddenly replaced the apparent agnosticism about the after-life revealed in the
Apology by a theory based entirely on a belief in the immortality of the soul? The reason in each case is the same: he
has evidently found in Pythagoreanism something which
he believes to throw light on those ethical problems which
he had inherited from Socrates and been discussing ever
since. I do not think that it is by any means safe to deduce
from this fact that between the *Gorgias* and the *Meno*
Plato had paid his first visit to Italy and Sicily, but the

hypothesis is attractive. *Epistle* VII suggests in at least two passages (338–9 and 350) that Plato and Archytas of Tarentum, the versatile Pythagorean who was not only mathematician and philosopher but also statesman and general, were on terms of friendship and mutual respect. As Taylor writes in a slightly different but related context (*op. cit.* p. 6),

If there is any truth in the statement that the real object of Plato's journey was to visit the Pythagoreans, who were beginning to be formed into a school again under Archytas of Tarentum, we may suppose that it was precisely the purpose of founding the Academy which led Plato just at this juncture to the very quarter where he might expect to pick up useful hints and suggestions for his guidance; but this can be no more than a conjecture.

The safest part of the conjecture would seem to be that at any rate Plato and Archytas became friends during Plato's first visit to the West, in which case there is a reasonably solid foundation for the further conjecture that Plato had now learnt at first hand a good deal more of the Pythagoreans' beliefs than he knew when he wrote the early group of dialogues.

But be that as it may, I believe it is no longer a mere conjecture but an almost irresistible conclusion from the *Meno* that the theory of Ideas first dawned on Plato's mind as the result of his reflection on what he had learnt, directly or indirectly, from the Pythagoreans. If, in a world in which we have never seen anything that is perfectly square or perfectly circular, we can nevertheless clearly visualize and exactly define the perfect square or the perfect circle, and if we can on this foundation build up a whole system of eternally true propositions, why should we not be able to do exactly the same in the field of ethics? Why should not perfect piety be on just the same footing as the perfect square? Why should we not be able to define perfect piety as precisely and formulate eternally true propositions about it too? And might it not, finally, have been just such entities as this which Socrates had been seeking in his constant quest for universal definitions? While the particulars of the world of sense are, as Heraclitus had said long ago, undergoing incessant change, these entities are eternally changeless; and so, while the particulars of the sense world can be the objects only of opinion, right or wrong, this other class of entities are the objects of knowledge.

These suggestions are not, of course, by any means original; most of them stem ultimately from Aristotle. In his discussions of the origins of the theory of Ideas Aristotle tells us that, though it owed much to the Heraclitean belief in universal flux, which Plato learnt from Cratylus, and much also to the Socratic search for ethical definitions, it owed most of all to the Pythagoreans, and especially to their doctrine that 'things imitate numbers'. That is a characteristically Aristotelian piece of cold analysis which, however accurate in detail, overlooks the cardinal fact that it required the genius of Plato to blend three such diverse elements into an inspired and inspiring unity. The *Meno* seems to throw a clearer and a warmer light on the same subject.

CHAPTER 6

THE ACADEMY

If my reconstruction of the first half of Plato's life is in
essentials accurate, then the *Meno* must have been written
at much the same time as the Academy was founded.
The following section of this book will be more concerned
with the development of Plato's philosophy than with
the events of his life. This, therefore, is the place to say a
little about the characteristics and the aims of the Academy. I alluded in Chapter 2 to the rivalry between Plato
and Isocrates, the heads of two very different educational
establishments. That rivalry affords the best introduction
to a few further details.

Isocrates, who was some years older than Plato, had
already opened his school by the time the Academy was
founded. Its aims were simple enough; he explains them
himself, first in *Against the Sophists*, 'which formed',
according to Gilbert Murray (*Ancient Greek Literature*,
p. 343), 'a sort of prospectus of his system', and again, when
he was over eighty, in his peevish defence of his life's work
entitled the *Antidosis*. He sought to impart to his pupils a
general but superficial culture, which he called 'philosophy', and to train them in writing essays on the lines
of his own political pamphlets. He hoped to reform
society by sending out into public life a succession of
young men whom he had imbued with his own capacity
for couching the pious platitudes of pan-Hellenic politics

in polished prose. There was a large demand at the time for any form of higher education and his influence was great. But Plato would naturally have had very little use for anything so shallow. Plato's own programme, as *Republic* VII shows, involved among other things a long and arduous mathematical discipline, which Isocrates in his turn would have thought better calculated to emasculate than to invigorate a future statesman's judgment. A statesman, Plato believed, in the sense which he had given to the word in the *Gorgias*, must, like Socrates himself, the only true statesman, have pondered deeply on the real purpose of life. A training in abstract thought was the first essential, and such a training was best initiated by mathematics. Two schools professing the same objective, the training of potential politicians, could hardly have been more fundamentally different than those of Isocrates and Plato.

The traditional story of the foundation of the Academy is derived from at least four almost equally unreliable sources. The details of the story, which are luckily irrelevant, vary quite widely, but in its barest outlines the usual version is as follows. Dionysius is said to have reached such a pitch of impatient irritation with Plato's presence in his court, and with his puritanical influence on Dion and others, that in the end he handed him over to the captain of a Spartan ship which was just leaving Syracuse with instructions either to murder him on the way or else to sell him into slavery when the ship reached Aegina. Incidentally, Aegina was at war with Athens at the time. By a happy chance a certain Anniceris, who had conceived a great admiration for him when Plato paid his ill-attested visit to Cyrene, happened to be in Aegina and narrowly succeeded in saving Plato's life with a ransom of twenty minae. When Plato returned safe to Athens, Anniceris generously refused repayment; the money was used instead to buy a garden in the grove of the hero Academus; the property was vested in a society and dedicated to the cult of the Muses and of their leader, Apollo. Here was founded, not long after the first of all European colleges for adult education, the prototype of all modern universities. It lasted for the best part of a millennium.

Not much is to be learnt from this romance. Most probably the Academy was indeed founded quite soon after Plato's return home, as an indirect method of achieving what he had failed to achieve directly, the conversion of rulers, actual or potential, to philosophy; and his return home can be fairly confidently dated around 388-7 B.C. What is more certain is that the Academy soon began to attract such men of distinction as the mathematicians Theaetetus and Eudoxus. And what is indisputable is that from its foundation until his death at the age of eighty-one Plato was its head. While continuing his own writing, the extent of which alone is sufficient proof of phenomenal industry, he also lectured to his colleagues and pupils, and stimulated and supervised their collective research. Some modern scholars have doubted whether in the latter half of his admittedly long life Plato, or indeed anybody else, could have achieved so much. Taylor for instance, to resort again to his invaluable but controversial study, maintains that 'the President of the Academy would for long enough after its foundation be far too busy to write' (*Plato: The Man and his Work*, p. 21) and believes that the only dialogue which Plato could conceivably have written in the twenty years following the Academy's foundation is the *Phaedrus*. The 'most philosophically advanced section of the *Republic*', he argues (*op. cit.* p. 20), 'was already written in the year 388-7, with the consequence that the *Republic*, and by consequence the earlier dialogues in general, were completed at least soon after Plato was forty and perhaps before foundation of the Academy'. This argument, however, merely shifts the same difficulty back from the latter to the earlier half of Plato's life. As Taylor himself says (*op. cit.* p. 21), the first of the 'two distinct periods of literary activity to be distinguished in Plato's life . . . cannot have begun before the death of Socrates', by which time Plato was already in his late twenties. The reconstruction outlined in this section certainly compels us to believe that while he was 'President of the Academy' Plato wrote, not only all those dialogues which are generally accepted as belonging to the late group, but also the *Meno*, the *Phaedo*, the *Symposium*, the *Republic*, and the *Phaedrus*. But, after all, he was 'President of the Academy' for almost exactly forty years. The alternative to this view is to suppose that, in the dozen or so years between the death of Socrates and his own first visit to the West, Plato had found the time to write, not only the whole of the early group, but also at least the first four of the major works just listed. Granted that Plato's industry must indeed have been phenomenal: one of the few

Greeks who may have exceeded it is his own pupil, Aristotle. But Taylor's hypothesis seems to put Plato in the superhuman class whereas the generally accepted hypothesis does not.

As was argued in the last chapter, there are grounds for regarding the *Meno* as the first of the middle group of dialogues. In the *Phaedo* and the *Symposium* the doctrines foreshadowed in the *Meno* are elaborated in different ways. In the *Republic* they are as fully and explicitly formulated as Plato's mistrust of the written word would ever have permitted. I believe that the *Phaedo* was written before the *Symposium*, that one main motive of the *Symposium* was to relieve the extreme asceticism of the *Phaedo* by a vivid picture of the aesthetic as opposed to the strictly intellectual aspect of the theory of Ideas, and that the *Republic* then gives us the required synthesis. That is the theme to be developed, in greater detail than has hitherto been necessary, in the next section of this book.

PART II

CHAPTER 7

'PHAEDO'

The *Phaedo* is the most inspiring and the most important of Plato's shorter works. It is concerned as a whole with a theme of universal and perpetual interest, the immortality of the soul. Plato, still fired by Socrates' death, brings to his description of the last hours of his friend's life all his many and varied gifts. No other dialogue reveals such sustained seriousness, with only brief pauses for relaxation, or so subtle a blend of intellectual argument with emotional appeal. At this stage in his life Plato was still a poet as well as a philosopher. Later on, not only are the poets expelled, in *Republic* x, from the ideal state, but the poetical strain gradually vanishes from Plato's writing until, in the *Laws*, little remains but a prosaic monologue. In the *Phaedo* both the philosopher and the poet are working with the utmost intensity; and though they are working for the time being to the same end, there are occasional indications of a future tension in Plato himself, a presentiment of the nineteenth-century conflict between religion and science. He had learnt already, and proclaimed in the *Gorgias*, that the philosopher cannot in this imperfect world be also a man of action. The *Phaedo* leaves the impression that he is now wondering whether the philosopher can afford to be a poet either.

One particular passage of the *Phaedo*, moreover, which Plato's art contrives to present as a mere interlude

(95e–102a), contains not only his final assessment of Socrates' unique contribution to philosophy but also the first formal statement of the theory of Ideas. These six or seven pages are among the most important that Plato ever wrote. Yet even as he wrote them he was still feeling his way forward. As I said earlier, we should not seek in Plato for any systematic exposition of his views. This passage is an excellent illustration of that warning because, even while it presents us with some of the conclusions that Plato has already reached, it throws out a number of dark hints of the future development of his thought.

A fundamental question concerning the *Phaedo* is whether or not it gives us an accurate account of the events (including the people present and their conversation) of the last day of Socrates' life. Professors Burnet and Taylor of course maintained that it does. The theory of Ideas, they argued, must therefore have been well known to Socrates and his Pythagorean associates, who would anyhow have been familiar with geometrical forms; consequently the Ideas are at one point (100b4) expressly called 'that much-mooted topic',[1] a theme familiar to everybody present; and so they concluded that the theory must have been constantly discussed in the Socratic circle. If they were right, what I have so far written must be misguided and misleading.

Before I summarize the opposing case, which fortunately has powerful support, an analysis of the argument of the dialogue as a whole will place the discussion in its

---

[1] ἐκεῖνα τὰ πολυθρύλητα.

context. In broadest outline the argument can be subdivided into five stages:

(1) There is first an introductory statement of the main thesis, which is essentially religious. Death, Socrates maintains, is really the achievement of the soul's independence, and that, as three considerations show, is what the philosopher is always seeking. He cannot be bothered to attend to his body, but is concerned only with his soul; the body and its appetites are forever interfering with his thought; the supreme objects of all his studies are absolutes rather than sensible things. The life of the philosopher is therefore a constant rehearsal of death (60b–69e).

(2) Next come three arguments for the immortality of the soul, all of which seem intended to be approximate range-finders:

(i) *The so-called 'argument from opposites'*. The world is made up of opposites, hot and cold, great and small, and so on. Now if a thing becomes bigger it must first have been smaller; and so, universally, whatever comes to be comes out of its opposite. Thus, just as there are pairs of opposites, there are also pairs of opposite processes of becoming. And if we then apply this generalization to the opposites life and death, we see that we recognize only one of this pair of opposite processes, which we call dying. But there must also be the other member of the pair, coming to life. So the ancient belief that the dead are born again is confirmed.

(ii) *The argument from the doctrine of 'recollection', supported by a new proof of the doctrine itself.* No two sensible things, such as sticks or stones, are ever equal; yet the sight of two sticks that only approximate to equality reminds us of perfect equality. We must therefore have known perfect equality in a previous existence; and in that case we must not only have existed before birth, we must also have possessed intelligence.

(iii) *The answer to the earlier question, How do we know that the soul at death is not simply dispersed like smoke?* Socrates' reply is to the effect that composite things are dispersed while the incomposite, if any such exist, are not; moreover, composite things are mutable, incomposite things immutable. But Ideas are immutable, particulars mutable; and again Ideas are intelligible, particulars sensible. There are thus two classes of things, the mutable and sensible, and the immutable and intelligible. Obviously the body belongs to the former class, the soul to the latter. Furthermore, the soul commands and the body obeys; but to command is the function of the divine, to obey the function of the mortal. On both grounds together, therefore, the soul would appear to be constant and divine, the body mutable and mortal. But since even bodies, or parts of them such as bones, last a very long time, souls must be almost imperishable (69 e–85 b).

(3) Simmias and Cebes raise important objections to the argument as it has so far been developed. Simmias puts forward what may be one of the variant Pythagorean views of the soul, the theory that it is a mere 'harmony' or 'attunement' of the bodily constituents; that when the physical elements are correctly proportioned soul automatically supervenes, but that when that proportion is appreciably deranged soul vanishes again.

Cebes suggests that, just as a man might during his life-time make and wear out a succession of many cloaks, so the soul might assume and wear out a succession of many bodies, but still finally die (85 b–91 c).

(4) Socrates deals first with the objection of Simmias, which is the easier to counter. He argues first, and validly *ad hominem* since Simmias has already subscribed whole-heartedly to the doctrine of 'recollection', that the theory that the soul is a mere 'attunement' of physical elements is incompatible with that doctrine; he next argues that, as every 'attunement', or proportion, is by definition deter-minate, it follows that no 'attunement' is more or less of an 'attunement' than any other and that since, therefore, every soul must, on this theory, be equally an 'attune-ment', there is no place left for goodness or badness; and he argues finally that the soul can control the body and its feelings and so cannot possibly be a mere by-product of the right proportions of its ingredients. Simmias quickly capitulates (91 c–95 a). That brings us to the beginning of the passage to be considered in greater detail. I will therefore suspend my summary and return to the problem raised by Burnet and Taylor.

Something has been said in Part I about the reasons for which many distinguished scholars have refused to accept the view that the theory of Ideas was already a familiar topic in the Socratic circle. Ross for instance, in the intro-duction to his invaluable edition of Aristotle's *Meta-physics* (pp. xxxiii–xlv), takes his stand against Taylor primarily on the explicit statement of Aristotle, already cited in chapter 3, that, whereas Socrates did not regard his universals as separable, Plato and his followers gave them a separate existence. In my view, that is much the most powerful argument yet adduced on either side. But there are several other substantial considerations to the same effect, of which I shall mention only three. The first is gratefully borrowed from Appendix 1 of G. M. A. Grube's book, *Plato's Thought*.

Grube argues that

of the five different occasions on which the theory of Forms is discussed in the *Phaedo* . . . a different aspect of the theory is brought out on each occasion:

(*a*) in 65d–66a we are made to understand that there *are* realities which the mind or soul grasps without the help of the senses.

(*b*) in 72e–76c: these are the realities which the mind knew before birth, and of which we are reminded through sense-perception, in so far as the particulars 'imitate' the Forms.

(*c*) 78c–80b: the absolute unchangeability of the Forms is emphasized, and their nature contrasted with the physical world.

(*d*) 100b–e: participation in the Forms is the cause of phenomena and of their qualities.

(*e*) 102d–105b: a further discussion of participation and a difficult distinction between properties and accidents derived therefrom.

To quote Grube's argument in full beyond that point would be premature. But I can already without anticipation endorse two of his conclusions which follow: that 'this surely appears to be a gradual explanation of the theory of Ideas, the more difficult problems coming last'; and that 'the impression of a carefully graded explanation of the theory is confirmed by the fact that the technical vocabulary seems to be graded in the same manner. . . . The words εἶδος and ἰδέα [the two most regular words for Ideas] are not used to indicate the Forms until 103e and . . . after that they are used freely.' I therefore accept also Grube's general conclusion that, if the theory of Ideas was indeed already familiar to Socrates and his intimate circle, then Plato has taken an unconscionable time in leading up to the crucial point at 100a. If that crucial point is not a new point, would Plato have chosen, especially in a dialogue nominally devoted to quite another subject, to introduce it so gradually?

Of the two other lines of thought which lead in the same direction, one is a matter of fact, the other a matter of opinion. The fact can be stated in one sentence. Plato takes the trouble, in the introductory conversation of the *Phaedo*, to mention and account for his own absence: 'I believe', he makes Phaedo say at 59b10, 'that Plato was ill.' This, the only passage in any dialogue in which Plato mentions himself by name, looks like a deliberate hint that the dialogue is not to be taken as a reliable re-production of the actual conversation.

The matter of opinion is naturally more controversial. If, as I believe, the theory of Ideas is indeed new, then Plato's artistry, of which the *Phaedo* is a supreme example, is surely adequate to conceal its novelty. The main topic of the *Phaedo* is the divinity and immortality of the soul. The Ideas, however important, are introduced merely to contribute to that topic. To draw attention to their novelty would be to distract attention from the main theme, which Plato would hardly have wished to do when the theme in question was so near to his own heart.

On these and other grounds I have no hesitation so far in siding with the majority of modern scholars against Burnet and Taylor. There is however one other argument of Taylor's which at first sight looks so convincing that it should be quoted. 'We are . . . bound', he writes (*op. cit.* p. 176), 'to accept his [Plato's] account of Socrates' conduct and conversation on the last day of his life as in all essentials historical, unless we are willing to suppose him capable of a conscious and deliberate misrepresentation recognizable as such by the very persons whom he indicates as the sources of his narrative.' What Taylor would regard as 'a conscious and deliberate misrepresentation' I should describe rather as an exceptionally graceful tribute. I believe that Plato, even while he knew that the theory of Ideas was his own discovery and thought that it solved all the familiar Socratic problems, yet recognized that he owed it primarily to Socrates' constant search for universal ethical standards and secondarily to the Pythagoreans, represented in the *Phaedo* by Simmias and Cebes. He therefore goes out of his way to show that the theory was ultimately due to the influence of Socrates. Seeing that the doctrine in question is the very heart of his own philosophy, I can think of no more generous ascription. The *Phaedo* is in at least one real and obvious sense Plato's final obituary of his master. He could hardly include in such an obituary, a dialogue in which Socrates holds the centre of the stage throughout, any direct reference to Socrates' posthumous influence. I confess that I am neither surprised nor shocked that he should have seen fit to include oblique references instead.

My analysis of the argument of the *Phaedo* has so far brought us to the point where Socrates, in an apparent digression, begins on his answer to the objection of Cebes. As the passage which follows must be discussed in greater detail than any so far cited, I shall summarize the first four pages but quote the remaining three in full. There is, however, one preliminary point to be made.

The view has been held by various scholars, and with various modifications, that the intellectual biography which Plato here gives us is not in fact, as it purports to be, the biography of Socrates so much as, in Hackforth's phrase, 'an impersonal sketch of philosophical development *in abstracto*' (*Plato's 'Phaedo'*, p. 130). And there is quite a lot to be said for at least one variant of this view. Plato divides Socrates' philosophical development into three separate stages. A student of early Greek philosophy might, in a very brief summary, divide the whole history of Greek thought down to the time of Socrates into three closely comparable stages. There was first the purely physical speculation exemplified by the Milesians; next came the stage, exemplified by Empedocles as well as Anaxagoras, when a moving cause of some sort or another had to be postulated; and finally Socrates himself directed men's gaze inwards from the universe around them on to their own souls. Some such view is attractive. I am tempted to believe that Plato included the first two

stages of the biography partly for the purpose of under-
lining the supreme importance of Socrates' contribution
to philosophy in contrast to that of his predecessors. He
was certainly capable of such an artifice. Not that he has
deliberately distorted the story of Socrates' development;
but he may have wished to stress those stages in Socrates'
life which would throw most light on the real significance
of his achievement. In that case he would in this passage
be doing on a small scale, and from a special angle, just
what he is doing on a large scale, and from several different angles, in the dialogue as a whole. Once again he
is consciously writing his final obituary of Socrates.

We now come to what Plato himself actually chooses
to tell us. In his youth, as he is made to say at the outset
of his 'autobiography', Socrates was engrossed in the
old speculations of the physicists. How do living creatures
develop? With what ingredient in us do we think? And
so on. But so far from learning in this way, as he had
hoped he would, 'the causes of everything, why each
thing comes into being, why it perishes, why it exists'
(96a9), he eventually found that he 'unlearnt' even what
he had till then thought that he knew (96c6). At that
stage, however—and here we pass to the second of the
three stages—'I heard somebody reading from a book
written, he said, by Anaxagoras to the effect that it is
Mind that ordains and causes all things' (97b8). This
greatly excited him, because he assumed that Anaxagoras
would go on to show how everything in the world was
arranged as it was, as it surely would be by Mind, because
it was best for it to be so. Accordingly 'I enthusiastically

got hold of the books and began to read them as quick as I could. . . . But from this wonderful hope I was at once dashed down' (98b4–7); for Anaxagoras, having once employed Mind to initiate motion, thereafter had recourse to the usual mechanical explanations. 'Fancy being unable to distinguish the real cause [i.e. the formal and final causes] from that without which the cause could never be a cause [i.e. the material cause]' (99b2). That confusion is analogous to saying that Socrates is now sitting in prison because his bones and sinews are so disposed rather than for the real reason, which is his mind or intelligence. So, thwarted in his hope that somebody would teach him, and unable by the study of particulars to discover for himself, how everything was arranged, as it should be, in the best possible way, Socrates moved on to the third stage. He himself calls it, presumably in relation to the kind of causation that he had hoped to learn from Anaxagoras, 'a second-best course' (99c9). But for all that, what follows is so vitally important that it must be quoted in full, starting at 99d4. And this time, instead of giving my own translation, I shall use that of Hackforth. I intend later to join issue with him on the significance of the crucial part of the passage and, in order to avoid any suspicion of distortion, will do so on his own terms. The sentences to be discussed presently are printed in italics and numbered in the order in which I shall discuss them.

'Well, at that point, when I had wearied of my investigations I felt that I must be careful not to meet the fate which befalls those who observe and investigate an eclipse of the sun; sometimes, I believe, they ruin their eyesight, unless they look at its image in water or some other medium. I had the same sort of idea: I was afraid I might be completely blinded in my mind if I looked at things with my eyes and attempted to apprehend them with one or other of my senses; so I decided I must take refuge in propositions, and study the truth of things in them. Perhaps, however, my comparison in one aspect does not hold good: for I don't altogether admit that studying things in propositions is more of an image-study than studying them in external objects. (3) *Anyhow, it was on this path I set out: on each occasion I assume the proposition which I judge to be the soundest, and I put down as true whatever seems to be in agreement with this, whether the question is about causes or anything else; what does not seem to be in agreement I put down as false.* But I should like to make my meaning clearer to you: I fancy you don't as yet understand.'

'Indeed, no,' said Cebes, 'not very well.'

'Well, here is what I mean; it is nothing new, but what I have constantly spoken of both in the talk we have been having and at other times too. I am going to attempt a formal account of the sort of cause that I have been concerned with, and I shall go back to my well-worn theme and make it my starting point; that is, (1) *I shall assume the existence of a beautiful that is in and by itself, and a good, and a great, and so on with the rest of them; and if you grant me them and admit their existence, I hope they will make it possible for me to discover and expound to you the cause of the soul's immortality.*'

'Why of course I grant you that,' said Cebes: 'so pray lose no time in finishing your story.'

'Now consider whether you think as I do about the next point. It appears to me that if anything else is beautiful besides the beautiful itself the sole reason for its being so is that it participates in that beautiful; and I assert that the same principle applies in all cases. Do you assent to a cause of that sort?'

'Yes, I do.'

'It follows that I can no longer understand nor recognise

those other learned causes which they speak of; if anyone tells me that the reason why such-and-such a thing is beautiful is that it has a bright colour or a certain shape or something of that kind, I take no notice of it all, for I find it all confusing, save for one fact, which in my simple, naive and maybe foolish fashion I hug close: namely that (2) *what makes a thing beautiful is nothing other than the presence or communication of that beautiful itself—if indeed these are the right terms to express how it comes to be there: for I won't go so far as to dogmatize about that, but merely affirm that all beautiful things are beautiful because of the beautiful itself.* That seems to me the safest answer for me to give whether to myself or to another; if I hold fast to that I feel I am not likely to come to grief; yes, the safe course is to tell myself or anybody else that beautiful things are beautiful because of the beautiful itself. Do you not agree?'

'I do.'

'Similarly big things are big, and bigger things are bigger, because of bigness; while smaller things are smaller because of smallness.'

'Yes.'

'Then you would reject, as I do, the assertion that one man is bigger than another by, or because of, his head, and that the latter is smaller by, or because of, that same thing; you would protest that the only thing you could say is that anything bigger than another thing is so solely because of bigness, that bigness is the reason for its being bigger; and again that a smaller thing is smaller because of smallness, and smallness is the reason for its being smaller. You would, I fancy, be afraid that if you said that someone was bigger or smaller 'by a head', you would be met with the objection that in the first place it would be by the same thing that the bigger is bigger and the smaller smaller, and in the second place that the head by which the bigger man is bigger is itself small; and that, it would be objected, is monstrous, for a big man to be big by, or because of, something small. Or wouldn't you be afraid of that?'

'Yes, I should,' replied Cebes with a laugh.

'Then would you be afraid to say that ten is more than eight by two, and that two is the cause of the excess, instead of saying by quantity and because of quantity? Or that a length of two yards is greater than a length of one yard by half its own length, rather than by greatness? Surely you should have the same qualms as before.'

'Quite so.'

'Or again, wouldn't you hesitate to say that when one is added to one the addition is the cause of there coming to be two, or that when one is divided the division is the cause? Would you not loudly protest that the only way you know of, by which anything comes to be, is by its participating in the special being in which it does participate; and that in the case just mentioned you know of no other cause of there coming to be two save coming to participate in duality, in which everything that is to be two must participate, just as anything that is to be one must participate in unity; all these divisions and additions and suchlike subtleties you would have nothing to do with; you would leave questions about them to be answered by wiser folk; conscious of your inexperience (4) *you would shy, as the phrase goes, at your own shadow, cling to the safety of your hypothesis, and answer accordingly. And if anyone were to fasten upon the hypothesis itself, you would disregard him, and refuse to answer until you could consider the consequences of it, and see whether they agreed or disagreed with each other. But when the time came for you to establish the hypothesis itself, you would pursue the same method: you would assume some more ultimate hypothesis, the best you could find, and continue till you reached something satisfactory. But you wouldn't muddle matters as contentious people do, by simultaneously discussing premiss and consequences, that is if you wanted to discover a truth.* Such discovery is perhaps a matter of complete unconcern to the contentious, whose wisdom enables them to jumble everything up together, and nevertheless to be well pleased with themselves.

But you, I fancy, if you are a philosopher, will do as I have said.'

'What you say', replied Simmias and Cebes together, 'is perfectly true.'

This passage, besides giving us the first explicit and reasonably full formulation of the theory of Ideas, is notable also for several other associated reasons. I will deal first with two general points which seem to me to be of the highest importance in that they provide the basis for my belief that the *Phaedo* was written, as is generally agreed, after the *Meno* and, which is more controversial, before the *Symposium*.

The first point to note is that the two separate strands of the *Meno*, the new and as yet somewhat confusing hypothetical method and the clear foreshadowing of the theory of Ideas, are here in the *Phaedo* no longer separate and apparently independent strands but have been woven together into one. 'I shall assume', says Socrates at 100 b 5 (or 'I shall take as my hypothesis'[1]), 'the existence of a beautiful that is in and by itself, and a good, and a great, and so on with the rest of them.' The theory of Ideas, in other words, has itself become the hypothesis from which Plato hopes to 'discover and expound . . . the cause of the soul's immortality'.

And second, in accordance with its being so far only a hypothesis, the theory is not yet fully elaborated. Plato himself says so almost in so many words. 'What makes a thing beautiful', Socrates says at 100 d 4, 'is nothing other than the presence or communion of that beautiful itself—

---

[1] ὑποθέμενος.

if indeed these are the right terms to express how it comes to be there: for I won't go so far as to dogmatize about that, but merely affirm that all beautiful things are beautiful because of the beautiful itself.' And if that sentence is not in itself sufficient proof of the present incompleteness of the theory, then we can turn on to another sentence a few pages later which conveys exactly the same impression in even more explicit terms. 'Our first hypotheses,' says Socrates of the Ideas at 107 b 5 (this time in my own translation), 'though they are acceptable to you, must be investigated more precisely; and if you divide them up adequately, you will, I believe, be following the argument as far as a man can.' The theory of Ideas is not yet worked out to its conclusion; the task of 'dividing up' the Ideas, here briefly recommended as a future duty, is taken in hand in certain later dialogues, notably the *Phaedrus* and the *Sophist*.

These two points, however important, do not call for lengthy elaboration. The next topic, the hypothetical method which Socrates describes in this passage as his own, does. There are two excerpts from the passage which tell us all we can yet learn of the method. The first begins at 100 a 3:

Anyhow, it was on this path I set out: on each occasion I assume [*or* take as my hypothesis[1]] the proposition which I judge to be the soundest, and I put down as true whatever seems to be in agreement with this, whether the question is about causes or anything else; what does not seem to be in agreement I put down as false.

[1] Again ὑποθέμενος.

The second begins at 101 c9:

You would . . . cling to the safety of your hypothesis, and answer accordingly. And if anyone were to fasten upon the hypothesis itself, you would disregard him, and refuse to answer until you could consider the consequences of it, and see whether they agreed or disagreed with each other. But when the time came for you to establish the hypothesis itself, you would pursue the same method: you would assume some more ultimate hypothesis, the best you could find, and continue until you reached something satisfactory. But you wouldn't muddle matters as contentious people do, by simultaneously discussing premiss and consequences, that is if you wanted to discover a truth.

I will first consider these two passages separately and then discuss their combined significance.

The first passage suggests that the hypothetical method in its new guise involves only two steps, though a third is fairly obviously implied in the phrase 'the proposition which I judge to be soundest'. First—and this is the step that is only implied—you survey all the possible hypotheses which might account for the things or facts to be explained. Second, you select the strongest of these. And third, you posit as true anything which that hypothesis implies and as false anything the contrary of which it implies.[1] The method thus briefly described is of course very familiar to us; it is the method of modern science. But Plato's first explicit description of it in this passage constitutes a remarkable innovation. It is, and was even

[1] In this sentence I am consciously simplifying what Socrates actually says. In common with many others I believe that this is what Plato must have meant.

in Plato's day, the method of mathematics. Its fundamental characteristic is that it is deductive; it works downwards from a premise to a conclusion. I suggested in my chapter on the *Meno* that the theory of Ideas owed its origin largely to mathematics. Concluding from his reflection on the subject that mathematics concerned, not the sensible, mutable and perishable particulars of this world, but the intelligible, immutable and eternal realities of another world, Plato extended this discovery from the mathematical into the ethical sphere; he postulated equally eternal and immutable ethical Ideas, the knowledge of which, by the Socratic definition, was identical with virtue. Here in the *Phaedo* Plato does exactly the same with his method: he extends a method hitherto confined to mathematics into the moral, the aesthetic and, ultimately, the metaphysical spheres. When described as a mere extension this may not sound very original. It is actually, however, one of Plato's most influential contributions to thought. The first step has been taken, and a big step, towards the so-called Platonic Dialectic, which was the prototype, formally developed by Aristotle, not only of all logic but of all scientific classification as well.

But so far we have been concerned with only half the method. The second excerpt has still to be considered. It falls into halves, the first of which merely paraphrases and in one way slightly amplifies the sentences we have just been considering. 'You would cling to the safety of your hypothesis [that is, the theory of Ideas as it has just been expounded], and answer accordingly.' You would, for instance, explain the beauty of Helen of Troy by the 'presence or communion' of Beauty itself. 'And if anyone were to fasten upon the hypothesis itself,' or, in other words, if anyone were to question the theory of Ideas, 'you would disregard him, and refuse to answer until you could consider the consequences of it, and see whether they agreed or disagreed with each other.' The first test of any hypothesis, including the theory of Ideas, is to see whether the consequences which, in your movement downwards, you can deduce from it are consistent one with another, and also presumably, though Plato omits to mention this, with what you have already learnt, by applying the same procedure to other topics, to be the truth. So far, in fact, the only new suggestion in this second excerpt is the possibility that the theory of Ideas might be questioned. Otherwise the procedure is just the same as in the first excerpt; by hypothesizing the Ideas you are enabled to 'give an account' of the particulars of the sensible world.

The next few lines however contain an entirely new suggestion. 'But when the time came for you to establish the hypothesis itself, you would pursue the same method: you would assume some more ultimate hypothesis, the best you could find, and continue until you reached something satisfactory.' Despite its brevity, this is a vitally important sentence, and one which has been repeatedly misunderstood. I shall therefore analyse it clause by clause.

'But when the time came for you to establish the hypothesis itself . . .' or more literally 'But when you had to give an account of the hypothesis itself, . . .'[1] Suppose,

---

[1] ἐπειδὴ δὲ ἐκείνης αὐτῆς δέοι σε διδόναι λόγον, ...

in other words, that just as hitherto you have been giving an account of particulars by reference to the Ideas, so you now have to give a similar account of the Ideas themselves. Whatever is there in heaven or earth to which, as to a higher cause, you can refer the Ideas? At first sight that may appear a startling question, and in consequence the natural and, to my mind, obvious significance of the passage is constantly overlooked. Editor after editor assumes that the Ideas, being for Plato the ultimate reality, cannot possibly be derived, as particulars are, from a higher reality. And so Plato's own answer, that 'you would pursue the same method: you would assume some more ultimate hypothesis, the best you could find, and continue until you reached something satisfactory', is drained of most of its meaning. The crucial words 'something satisfactory'[1] are taken, as they are by Hackforth (*op. cit.* p. 141), to mean 'a hypothesis to which the interlocutor can find no ground for objection or doubt'. And as far as the Greek goes, there is no reason at all why they should not mean just that and nothing more.

But, for all that, there is still an overwhelming objection to this interpretation, an objection which Hackforth seems wrong to evade. The hypothesis that you are called upon to defend is unquestionably the theory of Ideas as it has so far been expounded. This theory your interlocutor, who is no Platonist but an ordinary man in the street, refuses to accept—a situation which is easily imagined. You therefore proceed to deduce the Ideas from some still higher hypothesis, 'hypothesizing', in Plato's own words

[1] τι ἱκανόν.

literally translated, 'another hypothesis which seems best of those above', and you continue the process until you come to 'something satisfactory'. Now even if the word which Hackforth translates as 'more ultimate', and I, more literally, as 'above',[1] does not of itself convey the sense of 'more remote from particulars', yet the truth can only be that any hypothesis which 'gives an account' of the Ideas themselves is bound to be more remote; the higher the plane of reality on which your hypothesis rests, the more remote will it be. If, then, your interlocutor declines to accept your first hypothesis, the theory of Ideas, what hope can you have that by climbing to ever higher and more remote levels of reality, you will at last reach something which he may be prepared to accept? On the contrary, the higher the level of reality on which it rests, the less acceptable will your hypothesis be.

What, then, is the real significance of the passage? The question cannot be answered fully until we come to the *Republic*. But this much can be safely said already. Plato in the *Phaedo* is for the first time committing to paper an explicit formulation of the theory of Ideas, and in what he calls his 'second-best course' he is employing the theory primarily, and very nearly exclusively, to explain the causes of the particulars of the sensible world. It is a new theory. He does not as yet choose to give a final and comprehensive explanation of all that it implies. At the same time he seems to feel that the Ideas, true as they may be as an explanation of particulars, still constitute so

[1] The word ἄνωθεν, the significance of which in this particular context is often underestimated.

manifold and diversified a plurality that the theory in its present form may be incomplete. What, he asks himself, if someone refuses, possibly because it leaves this unexplained plurality and diversity, to accept the theory of Ideas? Then we must attempt to derive the Ideas themselves from something less manifold and diversified, and we must continue the process of hypothesizing higher and higher hypotheses until we eventually reach 'something satisfactory'. What this 'something satisfactory' may be he certainly does not yet tell us and possibly may not yet have discerned. The whole of what I shall call the upward movement of thought, the movement from the Ideas to yet higher levels of reality, seems to be an aspect of the theory which he has not yet worked out in detail. Accordingly we find that in the *Phaedo* it occupies a mere three lines of Greek; and instead of telling us, as he does in the *Republic*, that it leads to the Idea of the Good, he tells us only that it leads to 'something satisfactory'. But vague as that phrase is, I cannot myself believe that it means anything so relative or subjective as 'adequate to satisfy an objector'.

I have discussed this section of Socrates' 'autobiography', and especially these last two excerpts from it, in perhaps disproportionate detail because here for the first time are clearly foreshadowed all the later developments in the essential Platonism. The passage presents both a new metaphysic and a new method; and however much Plato later developed and expanded them, he never abandoned either. The new metaphysic of the *Phaedo*, namely the theory of Ideas, amounts so far to this: in the mathematical, ethical and aesthetic spheres, and perhaps in other spheres as well, there exists, underlying the changing and perishable particulars of the world of sense, an as yet undefined and indeterminate plurality of constant and eternal Ideas. These Ideas act, by some unknown relationship, as the causes of phenomena; a thing that is beautiful or large owes its beauty or its size to the 'presence or communion' of the appropriate Idea. Of the theory in its present form there are two points to be particularly noted. First, the extent of the world of Ideas is still undefined; granting that there are Ideas of Beauty, Equality and Bigness, what about Bed or Injustice or Dirt? And second, the relationship of Ideas to particulars is equally undefined. A fair objection to the theory in its present form might be that all that it has done is dogmatically to assert the independent existence of absolutes without attempting an explanation. Some indeed, who have no use for idealism, might go further and dismiss the crucial sentence, 'All beautiful things are beautiful because of the beautiful itself,' as a mere tautology. Anyhow, the theory is in both these ways still very vulnerable, as Plato himself saw. He devotes much attention later, especially in a section of the *Parmenides* which will be cited in due course, to these very two points.

As for the method, the other and inseparable aspect of the new theory, the *Phaedo* presents us with two movements of thought, a downward movement and an upward movement. Both alike start from the hypothesis of the Ideas. The downward movement proceeds, by deduction from the Ideas, to give an account of particulars.

The upward movement, by induction, moves up through ever higher levels of reality to 'something satisfactory'. The two movements are wholly distinct; Plato ends the passage with a warning against confusing them. 'You wouldn't muddle matters up as contentious people do, by simultaneously discussing premiss and consequences, that is if you wanted to discover a truth.' Of the two movements the *Phaedo* gives us a relatively full description and exemplification of the first, the downward movement; the second, for the reasons already given, is stated in an excessively summary fashion and not exemplified at all. But to conclude from this that Plato regarded the upward movement as secondary and unimportant would be rash indeed.

I will start my short conclusion to this chapter by resuming the analysis of the argument of the dialogue at the point that we have now reached.

The speech of Socrates which we have just been considering is immediately followed by a direct 'deduction' of the immortality of the soul. The argument is relatively long and complicated; a partial summary must suffice. There are some things, says Socrates, of which a particular Idea is essentially, as opposed to accidentally, predicated; snow for instance is essentially cold, Socrates only accidentally short. And such things, those with an essential quality, can never admit the opposite of that essential quality; snow will never admit the Idea 'warmth', but when warmth advances on it, the snow must either 'withdraw' or perish. Then, to apply these results to the soul, life is a necessary concomitant of the presence of soul as heat is of fire. Soul always brings life to any body in which it is present. But there is an opposite of life, namely death, and since life is an essential predicate of soul, it follows that death can never be predicated of it. Thus the soul is literally deathless; a dead soul is a contradiction in terms. So much, Socrates says at 105e8, has now been demonstrated, and there the final 'proof' ends. It is soon followed by a brilliantly imaginative myth of the fate of souls, good and bad, after their earthly life; and the myth is followed by the death scene.

We need not dwell on the fallacies on which all the *Phaedo*'s quasi-scientific arguments for immortality rest. The final proof is of course, like every intellectual proof of immortality ever offered, wholly inconclusive. To prove that there is no such thing as a dead soul is not to prove that the soul survives after the body has died. By Socrates' own admission about snow, the life of the soul must either withdraw when the body dies or else be anni-hilated. Plato's faith is that the former is true, but the emphatic 'So much has been demonstrated' may perhaps suggest that he himself, deep down, knew it to be only an article of faith, not scientifically proven. At least once before in the dialogue, at the stage where the objections of Simmias and Cebes have dashed the company from confidence into dejection, we can visualize Plato struggling to resolve an inner conflict. Is he to accept the Pythago-rean doctrine that man's soul has fallen from a state of bliss, whither it may return by studying and assimilating itself to the world's harmony? Or is he, still following

Socrates, to admit that such things lie beyond our knowledge because they do not admit of logical proof? And
now, at the end of the dialogue, the failure of this last
intellectual argument is followed by two inspiring appeals
to the emotions, the myth and the death scene. In the
Phaedo the intellectual agnostic eventually retires from the
field, leaving the religious poet in possession; and the poet,
having rounded off his myth with the simple words 'for the
prize is fair and our hope great', brings at the very end the
most powerful of all his weapons to bear on us. Already
several times, by subtle touches, Plato has reminded us
that Socrates, the best man of his time, is about to die.
The actual death scene, when it comes, is drawn with the
restraint of great dramatic art. The very last sentence of
all echoes the key of the whole scene: 'Such, Echecrates,
was the death of our friend, one who, we might well
claim, was, of all those of his time whom we have known,
the best and wisest and most righteous man.'

CHAPTER 8

'SYMPOSIUM'

Although the *Phaedo* leaves the poet in Plato victorious over the scientist, it does so only after a stern struggle. In the *Symposium* the poet is virtually unopposed. And whereas the *Phaedo*, despite its strong element of poetry, has a message of extreme asceticism, adopted by St Paul in the sentence 'I die daily', the *Symposium* is a vivid picture of warm and genial life. For pure pleasure, it is probably the most readable of all Plato's works; the only major dialogue to rival it for ease of reading is the *Phaedrus*. But for that very reason its philosophical importance, though very great, is confined to a small fraction of the whole. The central theme of the conversation is of course Eros, which, as preachers at weddings are apt to tell us, is one of three different Greek words denoting three different varieties of love. After the dinner is over, Eryximachus proposes that each member of the party should in turn deliver a eulogy on Eros, and they willingly comply. The six set speeches which follow occupy the greater part of the dialogue. We need seriously concern ourselves only with that of Socrates, which is not only the last but also much the longest.

There are two separate reasons why I am strongly inclined to date the *Symposium* between the *Phaedo* and the *Republic*, the first subjective and therefore disputable, the second, to my mind, neither. I will state both briefly now and try to substantiate the second and more cogent in the rest of this chapter.

The first reason is connected once again with the problem of what, if anything, we are entitled to conjecture about Plato's psychology, his motives and his development. On the question of the relative dates of the *Phaedo* and the *Symposium*, we are faced with a choice between conjectures. Did Plato merely accommodate his writing to his subject? Or did he feel, after he had written the *Symposium*, that it was altogether too earthy and fleshly a dialogue and therefore go on in the *Phaedo* to lay stress on the need of asceticism for the salvation of the soul? Or, finally, did he feel, after writing the *Phaedo*, that his proprietary brand of austerity was too bitter a pill for any but a few saints to swallow and therfore decide to coat it with a layer of sugar? To me the last conjecture is psychologically the most probable. But the objective arguments in favour of this view are often adduced on the other side. Both in the introduction to the dialogue, where Socrates is depicted as going into a contemplative trance on his way to the dinner, and in the final section, in which the drunken Alcibiades, bursting in on the party uninvited, launches into a long and factual eulogy of Socrates, Plato is evidently at pains to show that, however self-indulgent his companions, Socrates could still meet them on their own terms and drink or argue them under the table. For myself, I take these passages as Plato's suggestions that the good man, despite the *Phaedo*, will be ready to participate in the pleasures of this world but will nevertheless remain uncorrupted by them. Others will argue, perhaps with equal plausibility, that these same passages are designed to prepare the way for the rigours of the *Phaedo*.

Nobody will reach a firm decision on the basis of this consideration alone. The second consideration should carry more conviction. As we shall see, the ultimate objective of Socrates' brand of Eros was to gaze upon absolute Beauty itself. In the terms used in the last chapter, the eventual apprehension of absolute Beauty is, in the *Symposium*, the last step of all in the upward movement of thought. In the *Republic* absolute Beauty reappears in the guise of the Idea of the Good. The Good and the Beautiful, in other words, have replaced the 'something satisfactory' of the *Phaedo*. If Plato, at the time when he wrote the *Phaedo*, had already seen his way to the ultimate objective by the successive steps which he describes in the *Symposium* and the *Republic*, then, for some enigmatic reason, he must have decided that in the *Phaedo* the time was not yet ripe for the introduction of the supreme reality. Yet its introduction could have done nothing but strengthen his case for the immortality of the soul.

One of the chief subtleties of the *Symposium* lies in the various shades of meaning attached by the various speakers to the word Eros. To Phaedrus, who speaks first, it means nothing more nor less than sexual passion; for Socrates, who speaks last, it has left sexuality far behind. The intervening speeches, each doubtless geared to the individual character as well as to the profession of the speaker, gradually raise the tone of the conversation in preparation for the speech of Socrates. But even so, the moment Socrates begins to talk, the key alters abruptly. His conception of the nature and function of Eros is so much wider and deeper than that of any of the earlier speakers that, despite all Plato's artistry, the dialogue still falls into two main sections. Each of the first five speeches is designed as a preliminary to the speech of Socrates; each, whether by mere flippancy, as in the case of Aristophanes' eulogy, or by some graver defect, is carefully contrived to point the contrast with Socrates' earnest idealism. Plato is gradually preparing his reader for the gospel which he intends to preach, and in the process he is enjoying himself a great deal. Why not, indeed?

Phaedrus' identification of Eros with mere sex must have been, even for an ordinary Greek, a considerable over-simplification, because Eros had, after all, played a leading part in the earliest cosmogonies and must have long been credited with other characteristics besides simple sexuality. But for our present purposes we can afford to ignore all the other interpretations except Plato's own, which Socrates puts into the mouth of an otherwise unknown and most probably imaginary priestess called Diotima. Eros for Plato, strange as it may seem, is very closely akin to philosophy. Eros and philosophy are in fact two aspects of one and the same impulse: the impulse which drives a man's soul out to seek, and if he is lucky be united with, that to which it is akin. Such an impulse can, in Plato's view, be responsible for very different results, which we for our part might attribute to very different causes. It is responsible first for our love of our fellow human beings and our sympathy with them; so that Plato's Eros includes the Eros of Phaedrus, but only as a very small fraction. Next it is responsible for our appreciation of beauty, since our souls, so Plato would maintain, are attracted by the beautiful because they feel a kinship with it and repelled by the ugly because they feel it to be foreign to them. And it is responsible finally, and most paradoxically, for our intellectual curiosity, because our instinctive desire to understand and comply with our environment, as being again akin to it, is always urging us on to seek the truth. So each of three widely different qualities, human sympathy, aesthetic appreciation and intellectual curiosity, is for Plato the outcome of either Eros or philosophy. A passage at the beginning of *Republic* VI tells us that the philosopher, if he is defined as he should be as the 'lover of reality', must of logical necessity be, among other things, just and gentle as opposed to unsociable and savage. Similarly Diotima's speech, as we shall soon see, tells us that the true lover must love, among other things, the sciences. Just as absolute Beauty in the *Symposium* is the emotional counterpart of the Idea of the Good in the *Republic*, so the respective impulses which urge men on to seek these objectives, Eros and philosophy, are, for Plato, the emotional and the intellectual aspects of the selfsame impulse. That impulse is itself, as *Republic* VI again shows, nothing short of the character of the perfect man. The nearest parallel to this peculiarly Platonic conception is to be found, probably, in St Paul's description, in chapter 13 of the first Epistle to the Corinthians, of charity or love. This time, of course, the word for love is no longer Eros but another of the three, the characteristically Pauline word ἀγάπη.

But Plato's Eros and Paul's charity have many common characteristics. Just as Plato writes, yet again in *Republic* VI, of the Good and of the impulse which drives us to seek it, that it is (in Cornford's translation) 'a thing that every soul pursues as the end of all her actions, dimly divining its existence, but perplexed and unable to grasp its nature with the same clearness and assurance as in dealing with other things, and *so missing whatever value those other things might have*', so St Paul writes: 'Though I have the gift of prophecy, and understand all mysteries, and all knowledge; and though I have all faith, so that I could remove mountains, *and have not charity, I am nothing.*' And just as Plato's philosopher must be just and gentle, and his lover love *the sciences*, so 'charity suffereth long and is kind; charity . . . rejoiceth not in iniquity but rejoiceth in *the truth*'.

So much by way of preliminary to Socrates' contribution to the dialogue, which includes the speech of Diotima. And Socrates' contribution, like the dialogue as a whole, can without undue violence be divided into two sections, the first of which I shall only summarize, sometimes rather freely in order to bring out Plato's apparent point, but the second of which I shall translate in full and allow to speak for itself. In the original, whose tone is not easy to reproduce, it is unsurpassed in Greek prose writing.

Socrates starts, after a word of satirical praise for the high-sounding insincerity of the preceding speech by Agathon, the successful tragedian, by asking him a string of questions, nominally to find a starting-point for his own set speech but actually to make an important preliminary point which Agathon had altogether ignored. Eros, he argues, must be the desire for something which we do not possess; if we already possessed it we would have no need to desire it. If therefore, as Agathon readily admits, Eros desires beauty and goodness, it cannot already possess them. Although, however, love is not yet fair and good, it is not on that account, says Socrates, who is by now professedly quoting the priestess Diotima, to be dismissed as ugly and wicked either. There is a state between these extremes, just as there is between full knowledge and total ignorance, which can be expressed mythologically by describing Eros as neither a god nor a mortal but as a *daemon*, an intermediary between gods and men. Moreover, Diotima continues, his birth corresponds to his position. He is the son of Plenty and Poverty; he has inherited squalid poverty from his mother, persistent resourcefulness from his father. He is in fact, to come to the conclusion of this introductory section, the true philosopher—a conclusion, incidentally, which gives the weightiest possible authority to the close relationship, in Plato's view, between Eros and philosophy. Eros feels a hunger for wisdom, one of the fairest of all things, but he feels it only because it remains unsatisfied. Such, Plato means, is the conflict of the philosopher. Wisdom or knowledge is not an endowment of which men are automatically possessed; it is achieved only by incessant endeavour.

Having already complied with Agathon's insistence that a eulogy of Eros should deal first with its intrinsic character, Socrates passes next to its services to men.

Eros is really, he says, still quoting Diotima, nothing but the desire for happiness for ever. Strictly speaking, therefore, all men should be called 'lovers'. But just as all craftsmen, though they all make something, are not on that account called ποιηταί (meaning originally 'makers', but much more often 'poets'), so all lovers should not be called by that name, but the use of the word should be restricted to those who desire 'procreation in the beautiful'.

Now to interrupt Diotima for a moment, a traditional Pythagorean doctrine held that there are three types or grades of human life, represented allegorically by the hucksters who come to the Games to ply their trade there, the athletes who come to compete, and, far the highest of course, the spectators. Plato may well have been building on this allegory when, in the *Republic*, he divides the soul into the three parts which he calls respectively the appetitive, the spirited and the rational. Anyhow, this tripartite division, though it is not yet explicit, is clearly foreshadowed in the next section of Diotima's speech. For there are, she continues, three types of 'procreation in the beautiful', corresponding to the three divisions of the soul.

First of course, and corresponding to the appetitive part, there is the procreation of actual children, which is a universal and deep-seated instinct because it is merely a desire in the parent to perpetuate his own being. No mortal creature can realize this desire in its own individuality simply because it is mortal. But at least some sort of approximation to immortality can be achieved if the succession of generations is maintained. Indeed, it is this desire for eternity which makes each form of Eros, and especially the physical form, so very vehement.

Next, and corresponding to the spirited part of the soul, there is the passion for undying fame; and this, which is the motive of heroes, is just another and more spiritual form of 'desire for the eternal'. Just as the man who feels a craving for physical fatherhood is attracted by a woman, so the man whose soul is ready for the procreation of spiritual issue is attracted by 'a fair and noble and gifted soul'. If he is lucky enough to find such a one, he produces in union with it 'fairer and more deathless offspring', such as the poems of Homer or Hesiod, or the rules and institutions of Lycurgus or Solon.

And that brings us to the third and highest form of 'procreation in the beautiful', the form which corresponds to the rational part of the soul. Plato's description of this highest Eros, which I shall translate in full, begins at 209e5 and takes us to within about ten lines of the end of Socrates' speech:

Into these mysteries of love, Socrates, you might perhaps by your own effort have been initiated; but the consummation, the revelation, which is the aim, for one who seeks aright, of these early stages, I doubt whether you would have been able to attain. I will declare it to you myself, she said, with all zeal. Try to follow me if you can.

He who approaches the matter aright must begin to feel, while he is young, an attraction towards beautiful bodies; and he must first, if he who guides him guide him rightly, love one such body and engender therein beautiful thoughts. Next he should realize that the beauty in any one body is brother to the beauty in another, and that if he should pursue what is beautiful in form, it would be the height of folly not to consider the beauty in all bodies one and the same; and when he has taken this truth in, he should emerge as a lover of all beautiful bodies and abate his excessive love for one only, regarding it as trivial and contemptible. After that he should regard beauty in souls as more valuable than bodily beauty, so that one with an upright soul, even though with little beauty, would satisfy him as the object of his love and care, and he would seek to give birth to such thoughts as will improve the young. Thus he will be compelled to gaze at the beauty that there is in customs and laws, and to see the kinship of all this beauty; and so he will have come to regard bodily beauty as a trivial thing. And after customs he should lead his pupil on to the sciences, so that he may behold their beauty in turn, and, looking at the great breadth of beauty now attained, may no longer be enslaved like a servant, in his affection for the beauty of one boy or man or one institution, to a single beautiful thing, and so become petty and narrow-minded; rather he would turn to the great ocean of beauty, and, contemplating the many beautiful and noble thoughts therein, would give birth to his notions in ungrudging philosophy; until, there strengthened and enlarged, he glimpses a single such science, the science of universal beauty.

Now try, she said, to attend to my words to the utmost of your ability. He who has been trained thus far in the affairs of love, contemplating beautiful things in their right order, is now approaching the end of the study of love. He will suddenly glimpse a beauty that is wonderful in its nature—that very thing, Socrates, for the sake of which he undertook all his earlier toil. First, it is eternal; it is neither generated nor destroyed; it neither grows nor wastes away. Next, it is not beautiful in one aspect and in another ugly, nor beautiful at one time and not at another, nor beautiful in one relation and ugly in another, nor beautiful to some and ugly to others. Nor again can this beauty be pictured, like a face or hands or any other bodily part, or like a doctrine or a science. It never subsists in anything else—in a living thing, for instance, or in earth or heaven or anywhere else; it is in and by itself, eternally uniform. All other beautiful things partake of it in such a manner that, while all else is generated and destroyed, it alone never grows greater or less or is in any way affected.

When anyone, ascending from these first steps by a right course of love, begins to glimpse that absolute beauty, he can almost touch the consummation. For this is the right approach to the affairs of love, or the right way to be guided by another; to begin from particular objects of beauty and, for the sake of that absolute beauty, to climb on and on, as if on the rungs of a ladder, from one to two, from two to all beautiful bodies; from beautiful bodies to beautiful customs; from customs to beautiful branches of knowledge; so that, from beautiful branches of knowledge, one may end up at that branch of knowledge which is the knowledge of nothing other than this absolute beauty, and may understand in the end what absolute beauty is. Such is the life, my dear Socrates, said the stranger from Mantinea, which above all others a man should live, in contemplation of beauty itself. If you ever behold beauty itself, you will not class it with money, clothes, beautiful boys and young men, even though now, at sight of them, you are infatuated and ready, like many another, so long as you can see your beloved and be forever with him, neither to eat nor drink but only to gaze at him and be with him. What then, she said, do we think about anyone to whom is granted the sight of beauty itself, absolute, pure and uncontaminated; not immersed in human flesh or colour or other such mortal trivialities, but the divine and uniform beauty itself? Do you think a man's life would be paltry, she said, while he gazes thither and contemplates and associates with that for which we should strive? Do you not rather imagine that there alone will it befall him, while he sees beauty as it should be seen, to give birth, not to images of goodness, since he is not in contact with an image but with reality, but to true goodness? And when he has given birth to true goodness and reared it, then it is his lot to become dear to the gods and, if such is ever granted to any man, to become himself immortal.

This remarkable passage contains, in the original Greek, certain stylistic peculiarities, such as the studied repetition of various words and phrases, which make it very difficult, if not impossible, to render into natural English. Anybody who attempts to translate it will be left with a feeling of inadequacy. Shelley's version, for instance, achieves grandeur at the expense of frequent liberties with the Greek; my own, like most others which try to be fairly literal, sounds flat and uninspired. But the meaning of the original passage as a whole is not in doubt, and anybody who reads it is bound to feel that Plato was a mystic to whom were accorded experiences which are denied to the ordinary run of men.

What the passage contains is Plato's own narrative, put by his Socrates into the mouth of Diotima, of the pilgrimage of the soul from the moment when it first becomes conscious of its need to the moment of final consummation. Between the beginning and the end of the pilgrimage there are several stages, which Plato explicitly likens to the rungs of a ladder; the true 'lover', he maintains, is moving steadily upwards from one rung to the next. The pilgrimage begins at the early stage in a man's life when Eros first drives him out in search of that to which he feels himself akin; thereafter each successive level in his ascent will embrace all the earlier levels. The last of the three stages of what Plato calls 'procreation in the beautiful' will in fact embrace rather than exclude the earlier two. But at the same time, so far from regarding either of these earlier stages as final, as he might have done when he was still on the appropriate lower rung, the pilgrim who has succeeded in climbing to the top rung will regard them merely as the lower sections of a ladder which extends far above them. This is the aspect of Diotima's speech which is liable to misinterpretation. No doubt the lower rungs, when seen from the topmost, do look very low indeed. But to suppose that Plato believed that, once the pilgrim has climbed above them, he should thenceforward regard them as beneath contempt is to overlook the fact that, even in the *Symposium* itself, the guide who is to initiate the young into the mysteries of love assumes his responsibilities while his pupil is still on the lowest of all the rungs of the ladder. The objective of the whole ascent is not to blind ourselves to those parts of life which are relatively trivial; on the contrary, it is to integrate life and to enable us to see it whole. The *Republic* affords proof enough of that; this particular misconception is the outcome of studying the *Symposium* in isolation from the rest of Plato's writings. Physical love is, beyond any question, the first rung of Diotima's ladder. If it is regarded, not as an end in itself, but merely as the first step towards a higher end, it should never be forgotten as worthless but remembered with gratitude as the beginning of the initiation into higher mysteries.

The ascent which Diotima describes, although necessarily consisting of a succession of steps, is intended, of course, as a continuous progression. But we can still without undue violence divide it into two main stages. In the first stage, which begins with the love of a single beautiful body and ends with the love of fair 'customs[1] and laws', the pilgrim is still within the confines of this concrete and sensible world. At the moment, however, when he passes on from 'customs and laws' to 'sciences' or 'branches of knowledge', he is, in Plato's view, passing from the sensible to a supersensible world, in which he will remain until the final consummation is achieved. To force such a division on Diotima's speech may well seem arbitrary. Yet when it is so divided, this one speech, or even the one section of the speech which I have translated, serves as a summary introduction to the greater part of the *Republic*. The *Republic* must have been written soon after the *Symposium*. Not only does it give us, as I said earlier, the required synthesis between the austerity of the *Phaedo* and the warmth and colour of the *Symposium*; it also gives us, in a much more leisurely and detailed fashion, an account of the intellectual ascent which precisely corresponds to the emotional ascent already described by Diotima.

[1] ἐπιτηδεύματα = 'institutions', 'avocations', 'practices'.

CHAPTER 9

'REPUBLIC' I–VI

The *Republic* is in every sense so great a work, and covers
so wide a range of important topics, that an adequate
analysis of its argument is an impossibility. More than
any dialogue so far discussed it cries out to be read in full.
And fortunately since 1941, when Cornford's translation
first appeared, that task can be easily and enjoyably done;
here for once is a translation that is both natural and in all
essentials faithful. As Cornford himself admitted in his
witty preface, he did make certain abridgments; in his
own words (p. vii), 'the convention of question and
answer becomes formal and frequently tedious', and for
easy reading is usually best eliminated. Nevertheless,
when we come later on to the detailed analysis of certain
key passages, I shall sometimes attempt to forestall criticism by giving, at the expense of readability, a fuller and
more literal rendering.

Cornford's version also performed a minor and inci-
dental service. By the novel expedient of dividing the
dialogue into six Parts, he threw an immediate light on the
structure of the work as a whole. To quote another sentence from his preface (p. v), 'the traditional division into
ten "books", i.e. papyrus rolls, has been discarded, as an
accidental expedient of ancient book-production, having
little more to do with the structure of the argument than
the division of every Victorian novel into three volumes

had to do with the structure of the stories'. In this and the next chapter I shall gratefully accept Cornford's division of the *Republic* into six Parts rather than into ten Books.

If for the moment, then, we ignore Cornford's last three Parts, which together comprise only the last three Books and which are anyhow partly in the nature of appendices, the *Republic* falls into three main sections. Part I, which by a happy chance coincides exactly with Book I, is a characteristically Platonic introduction on the nature of justice. Indeed it bears so marked a resemblance to a typical sample of the early group of dialogues that certain scholars have argued that it must once have been intended as a separate short dialogue on its own and was only later in Plato's life made to serve as the introduction to a work of a very different scale. Be that as it may, Plato's motive in this introduction is plain enough; it is a motive which is discernible again, for instance, at a crucial stage in Book VI. He wishes at the outset to air, to refute, and so to dismiss from further consideration, certain current views, and notably the sophistic view, of the nature of justice.[1] Thrasymachus in *Republic* I is simply another Callicles. Plato has dealt with Callicles in the *Gorgias*. The introduction to the *Republic* skilfully anticipates the objections which Plato knows only too well are liable to be raised against the teaching of the rest of the dialogue.

Part II, which comprises Books II, III, IV and most of V,

[1] The precise meaning of the Greek words usually rendered 'just' and 'justice' is perhaps better conveyed by the biblical 'righteous' and 'righteousness'.

amounts essentially to a treatise on primary education. It opens with urgent requests from Glaucon and Adeimantus that Socrates show not only that justice is profitable, for the rewards it brings in its train, but that it is also intrinsically good. Socrates thereupon, on the ground that it is easier to see something delineated on a large scale than on a small, offers to describe his own ideal state; this will enable us to see wherein justice truly lies, and we can then apply our findings to the individual. And so, less than half-way through Book II (368e), we are launched on to the main theme. Unfortunately for his subsequent reputation among students of political theory, Plato deals first, in summary fashion, with the artisans, the shopkeepers, and the merchants. He is not in fact concerned with them at all; they are included only because he realizes that no state can exist without them. His real concern is with the Guardians, to whom he accordingly passes as soon as he decently can. We are still not far beyond the middle of Book II when Plato, having again dismissed a vast subject with which for the present he does not wish to concern himself, turns to his chosen topic. The rest of Part II, devoted to the primary education of the Guardians, presents a detailed account of the first stage of the pilgrim's progress of the *Symposium*. It describes first how the Guardians, by being brought up in a beautiful environment, shall gradually learn the kinship of all physical beauty and shall so begin to love beauty while hating and avoiding ugliness. Next we learn how they will come to value beauty of soul higher than mere physical beauty. And finally we are told how, by this upbringing, they will learn to love, and so to observe and enforce without as yet fully understanding, beautiful laws and customs. Thus we are instructed in the inculcation of right belief, which is all that the sensible world can ever admit, as opposed to the knowledge which is to be the theme of Part III. Since knowledge rather than right belief is our present concern, there is no need to linger over Part II. And moreover Plato himself, in the middle of Book III, has considerately given his readers a summary of the aims of his primary education which provides us, in three brief excerpts, with all the information needed for our present purposes. As in this instance Cornford's version involves no abridgment, I shall quote it verbatim.

The first excerpt begins at 401 b 8 and runs as follows:

We would not have our Guardians grow up among representations of moral deformity, as in some foul pasture where, day by day, feeding on every poisonous weed they would, little by little, gather insensibly a mass of corruption in their very souls. Rather we must seek out those craftsmen whose instinct guides them to whatsoever is lovely and gracious; so that our young men, dwelling in a wholesome climate, may drink in good from every quarter, whence, like a breeze bearing health from happy regions, some influence from noble works constantly falls upon eye and ear from childhood upward, and imperceptibly draws them into sympathy and harmony with the beauty of reason, whose impress they take.

There could be no better upbringing than that.

Hence, Glaucon, I continued, the decisive importance of education in poetry and music: rhythm and harmony sink deep into the recesses of the soul and take the strongest hold there, bringing that grace of body and mind which is only to be found in one who is brought up in the right way. Moreover, a proper training in this kind makes a man quick to perceive any defect or ugliness in art or in nature. Such deformity will rightly disgust him. Approving all that is lovely, he will welcome it home with joy into his soul and, nourished thereby, grow into a man of a noble spirit. All that is ugly and disgraceful he will rightly condemn and abhor while he is still too young to understand the reason; and when reason comes, he will greet her as a friend with whom his education has made him long familiar.

There, for all to see, is the first step in the pilgrim's ascent; not only the recognition of the kinship of all physical beauty but also the realization that the soul too is in some way akin to it and alien to ugliness. Eros has now fulfilled its first function for the Guardians.

Little more than half a page later we reach the second step in the ascent, the gradually dawning awareness that in comparison with beauty of spirit mere physical beauty is of little worth. This is how Plato expresses it:

And for him who has eyes to see it, there can be no fairer sight than the harmonious union of a noble character in the soul with an outward form answering thereto and bearing the same stamp of beauty.

There cannot.

And the fairest is also the most lovable.

Of course.

So the man who has been educated in poetry and music will be in love with such a person, but never with one who lacks this harmony.

Not if the defect should lie in the soul; if it were only some bodily blemish, he would accept that with patience and goodwill.

So much for the first two steps in the ascent. But the vital passage in this section of the *Republic* comes in the short gap between these two excerpts. Here it is:

Then, is it not true, in the same way, that we and these Guardians we are to bring up will never be fully cultivated until we can recognize the essential Forms of temperance, courage, liberality, high-mindedness, and all other kindred qualities, and also their opposites, wherever they occur? We must be able to discern the presence of these Forms themselves and also of their images in anything that contains them, realizing that, to recognize either, the same skill and practice are required, and that the most insignificant instance is not beneath our notice.

So Plato describes, in one short paragraph, the ultimate aim of his primary education. The objective is, in a more literal translation, the ability to 'recognize the forms of temperance, courage, liberality, high-mindedness and all kindred characteristics—and equally the opposites of these—as they move around all over the place,[1] and to discern their presence, and also that of their images, in everything in which they are present'.[2]

Unfortunately this last excerpt is by no means as simple as it may appear. This is the only passage in the whole of Part II where the Ideas are apparently mentioned, and Plato's real meaning in this one passage is far from clear. Admittedly the Ideas of temperance, courage and the rest are familiar enough to anybody who has read the *Phaedo*, and their 'images' are presumably therefore to be taken as their imitations in the sensible world. According to the

[1] πανταχοῦ περιφερόμενα.   [2] ἐνόντα ἐν οἶς ἔνεστιν.

orthodox interpretation of this passage, then, we have to learn to recognize both the Ideas and their images 'as they move around all over the place' and to 'discern their presence in everything in which they are present'. But any such interpretation poses great difficulties. As is later explicitly stated in the *Parmenides*, the Ideas do not 'move around', nor are they themselves, but only their 'images', to be found anywhere in the sensible world. On the contrary, each Idea is by definition unique, immutable and motionless. The orthodox interpretation, therefore, tacitly accuses Plato, at a crucial stage in his argument, of writing with a regrettable laxity.

There is, however, another interpretation available. Although the word εἴδη, which Cornford renders as 'Forms', is one of the two most regular words for the Ideas, Plato continued to use it, whenever it suited him, in other non-technical senses; indeed he was always at pains to avoid his writing hardening into a technical vocabulary. And one of the regular senses of the word, especially frequent in Plato, is that of 'class, kind' (see Liddell and Scott, *s.v.* III). That, I believe, must be the meaning of the word in the present context. Unless he has momentarily abandoned the firmest of his convictions Plato must here be speaking, not of his own Ideas, but of the old Socratic universals, which existed, as Aristotle tells us, only as embodied in the particulars of the sensible world. We must learn to recognize, this passage tells us, both the whole class of courage—or in other words that all courage, like all beauty, is akin—and its various exemplifications. Indeed, unless what we call courageous acts are a class united by certain common characteristics, we cannot be using words correctly; it would be absurd to call acts with no common characteristics by the same name.

This interpretation, even if unorthodox, has two great advantages. In the first place, if we are here concerned with the Socratic universals rather than the Platonic Ideas, then clearly, as Plato says, they do move around and they are embodied in the particulars of the world of sense. And in the second place, we can now account for the fact, already mentioned, that this is the only passage in the whole of Part II where the Ideas apparently figure at all. If, as I believe, they do not figure in this solitary passage either, then it appears that they are totally excluded from this whole Part. That fact is in itself so surprising, especially as the dialogue was probably composed quite soon after the *Phaedo*, that it calls for an explanation. Clearly it is no mere accident; on the contrary, it is the deliberate corollary of the very careful construction of the *Republic* as a whole. Part II, as we have seen, is concerned exclusively with right belief; it is designed to show just how far right belief, when properly trained, can carry us. But the Ideas are the object, not of belief, which is essentially concerned with particulars, but of knowledge. It is therefore vital to Plato's purpose altogether to exclude the Ideas from Part II. Otherwise the essential contrast between Part II, the essay on right belief, and Part III, the essay on knowledge, will be blunted. Indeed on this consideration alone I should be prepared to maintain that, in his description of the aims of primary education, Plato did not intend us to see the Ideas. Primary education is to teach the Guardians to recognize, first, the kinship of all physical or sensible beauty; second, the superiority of spiritual beauty over sensible; and third and last, not only individual acts of justice, temperance or courage, but also the characteristics which the members of each such class have in common. In a word, it is to carry them from the beginning of the pilgrim's progress of the *Symposium* as far as, but no further than, the love of 'beautiful laws and customs'.

So we come to the upper half of the pilgrimage, which is our real concern. Plato himself passes to it at Book v, 471. The ideal state as it has so far been described has been guided entirely by right belief as opposed to knowledge. The Guardians, in other words, though they are so disciplined as always to act aright, have as yet no knowledge of why they should act as they do; they have yet to achieve what Plato in the *Meno* called 'thinking out the reason why'. But at the same time, if they are indeed to be educated aright, as has so far been tacitly assumed, there must clearly be somebody in the state who possesses real knowledge to guide those who still lack it. Otherwise there would be no guarantee that the belief on which the Guardians have been fostered is indeed right rather than false belief. Part III accordingly opens, after a brief transitional passage to secure continuity, with the famous Platonic 'paradox' (Plato's own term for it) that (473 c 11): 'Unless philosophers become kings of states or else those who are now called kings and rulers become real and adequate philosophers . . . there can be no respite from evil either for states or, I believe, for the human race.'

Whence it follows, of course, that our own ideal Republic must be under the rule of a philosopher-king. And so our next task must be to determine exactly what we mean by a philosopher; until we know that, we cannot possibly devise an education calculated to produce him. The attempt at a definition actually occupies the rest of Book V, and the desired conclusion is reached on the last page. Philosophers, or lovers of wisdom, are there contrasted with 'lovers of seeming'. The latter are defined, at 479e 1, as 'those who look at many beautiful things but do not see Beauty itself, nor can follow another's guidance to it, or those who see many just things but not Justice itself, and so on in all cases'. The Guardians as they have so far been educated are in fact mere 'lovers of seeming', while 'philosophers' or 'lovers of wisdom' are defined at 480a 11 as 'those who, in each case, love the reality', or in other words the Ideas.

How then—and here we encounter the question which is to occupy us until the end of Part III—are we to train such lovers of Ideas? First, of course, we must select the right pupils for such a training, and Book VI therefore opens with a description of the character required in the potential philosopher. This is the passage already cited in the last chapter to show that Plato's philosopher is really nothing less than the perfect man, uniting in his person every conceivable human virtue. Given such material (though we may well wonder where to find it) we can set to work to train it for its task. But before he embarks on his programme of higher education, Plato launches first, quite naturally in the context although it is still a digression from his main theme, into a long and vivid defence of philosophy. The passage, which speaks eloquently for itself, is not strictly relevant to this discussion and must be omitted. It actually serves a double purpose. First, it answers the obvious objection which a reader might raise at this juncture, that philosophers in practice, so far from being the perfect men just described, are at best useless and at worst pernicious; and as a result it justifies Plato in resuming and completing his account of the ideal Republic.

The return to the main theme, which comes at 502c9, is clear enough. 'Now that this subject', says Socrates of the defence of philosophy, 'is eventually concluded, it remains to consider how, and by what studies and practices, the saviours of our republic will come into being'— a question which carries us to near the end of Book VII— 'and at what ages they should tackle each'—the question which occupies the remaining pages of that Book. This sentence amounts in fact to the table of contents which introduces what is perhaps the most celebrated passage in the whole of Plato, the Essay on the Good. That essay itself consists of three great analogies or allegories, the Sun, the Divided Line and the Cave. The three together contain as much of Plato's profoundest thought as, with his mistrust of the written as opposed to the spoken word, he ever consented to commit to paper. I shall deal with each of them in detail in the next chapter; and in the hope of illuminating their significance in advance, I end the present chapter with a summary paragraph on the place occupied, not only in Plato's writings but in Greek philosophy in general, by the conception of the Good.

The Good in Greek philosophy is, like Eros, a much wider term than we might expect. Plato again here, as he did in the *Symposium*, treats as inseparable three notions which may well seem to us to be entirely unconnected. The Good, for Plato, is first and most obviously the end or aim of life, the supreme object of all desire and all aspiration. Second, and more surprisingly, it is the condition of knowledge, that which makes the world intelligible and the mind intelligent. And third and last and most important, it is the creative and sustaining cause of the whole world and all its contents, that which gives to everything else its very existence. Nobody who comes for the first time to these three great allegories can hope for much understanding of them unless he realizes that Plato is attaching this triple significance to the word 'Good'. Here therefore, in a single cumbrous sentence, is the essence of Plato's beliefs on the subject. The Good, being that end or function for the fulfilment of which a thing exists, gives to a thing, whether natural or artificial, both its intelligibility (since the only way to understand a thing is to understand its function) and its reality (since only in fulfilling its function is it really what it is). So much by way of introduction to the analogy of the Sun.

CHAPTER 10

SUN, DIVIDED LINE AND CAVE

Although the analogy of the Sun does not begin until some five pages after Plato's return from his defence of philosophy to his main theme, those five pages themselves raise a number of points that are too important to be altogether omitted. Almost immediately after Socrates has formulated, in the sentence quoted in the last chapter, the two questions that are to occupy the remainder of Part III, he starts on the discussion of the first question, through what studies and practices philosopher-kings will come into being, by pointing out that they will inevitably be few and far between. Not only will they require all the moral qualifications already demanded of the Guardians in Part II; they will need also the intellectual qualification of aptitude for 'the highest studies'. So the question naturally arises, and is actually put twice before Socrates will answer it (504a2 and e4), What are these highest studies, or what is the one highest study of all? Socrates eventually replies, at 505a2, that 'the highest study' (or, in Cornford's version, 'the highest object of knowledge') 'is the Idea of the Good'.[1] And there for the first time we come face to face with the Idea of the Good. But that answer, Socrates continues, is itself inadequate because it merely gives rise to the further question, What is the Good? To that question, he says, two answers are readily

[1] ... ἡ τοῦ ἀγαθοῦ ἰδέα μέγιστον μάθημα.

forthcoming, the answers respectively of the masses and of the intelligentsia. Most people equate the Good with pleasure, a few with knowledge. But obviously it cannot be pleasure, since everybody would admit that some pleasures are bad. And equally it cannot be knowledge either, since, if the legitimate question were put, knowledge of what? the only possible answer would be, knowledge of the Good, which leaves the original and fundamental question still to answer. So once again, as he did in Book I, Plato carefully clears the ground of the most popular misconceptions before beginning to elaborate his own views.

The analogy of the Sun is itself introduced by a short but important passage beginning at 506 d 2. This is one of the few occasions in the dialogues where Plato tells us, almost in so many words, that he is not prepared to put his innermost and profoundest thoughts in writing. Here again is Cornford's rendering of it, which again involves no abridgement.

No really, Socrates, said Glaucon, you must not give up within sight of the goal. We should be quite content with an account of the Good like the one you gave us of justice and temperance and the other virtues.

So should I be, my dear Glaucon, much more than content! But I am afraid it is beyond my powers; with the best will in the world I should only disgrace myself and be laughed at. No, for the moment let us leave the question of the real meaning of the Good;[1] to arrive at what I at any rate believe it to

---

[1] Cornford here translated τἀγαθόν as 'good', without the definite article and with a small letter. This is the one alteration I have made in his version.

be would call for an effort too ambitious for an inquiry like ours. However, I will tell you, though only if you wish it, what I picture to myself as the offspring of the Good and the thing most nearly resembling it.

Well, tell us about the offspring, and you shall remain in our debt for an account of the parent.

I only wish it were within my power to offer, and within yours to receive, a settlement of the whole account. But you must be content now with the interest only;[1] and you must see to it that, in describing this offspring of the Good, I do not inadvertently cheat you with false coin.

We will keep a good eye on you. Go on.

And thereupon we reach the beginning of the analogy proper.

Before Plato breaks into new territory, he starts on ground which, from the *Phaedo* onwards, is familiar enough; the distinction is again drawn between many particulars, such as many men or many courageous acts, and the single underlying Idea of Man or of Courage. The former, says Socrates, are the objects of the senses, the latter can be apprehended only by thought. This is what Plato writes, very literally translated:

We must first reach an agreement, I said; I must first remind you of what we said earlier and what has often enough been said before.

What? he asked.

We maintain, said I, that there are many beautiful things, many good and so on in each case. These we distinguish in our thought.

Yes, indeed.

[1] A pun on the two meanings of the word *tokos*—'offspring' and 'interest' (on a loan).

At the same time we postulate Beauty itself and Goodness itself, and so on with everything which in the first case we postulated as many; we now class them under one Idea, on the ground that there is only a single Idea of each such class, and this Idea we call the reality of each.

That's true.

And we maintain that the many can be seen but not understood, while the Ideas can be understood but not seen.

Yes, certainly.

With what factor in our make-up do we see what is to be seen?

With our sight, he said.

And likewise, I went on, we perceive sounds with our sense of hearing and all other sensible things with our other senses?

Of course.

So far there is nothing new; but in the next part of the analogy we move at once on to fresh ground. The sense of sight, Plato continues, differs from all our other senses in that it alone requires a third factor, namely light, to act as a medium between the sense organ and the object perceived. Incidentally, Plato's later theory of sight is to be found in the *Timaeus*, 45 b–d. It is there expressed in rather complicated terms, but in its simplest outline it involves a quantity of pure fire enclosed in the eyeball, which flows out like to like in daylight and so effects sight, but at night flows out unlike to unlike and is so extinguished. Most probably some such theory underlies the present passage, but it is not necessary so to suppose. All that Plato is here wishing to emphasize is the simple fact that man cannot see in darkness. Moreover light, which is thus indispensable to sight, comes from the Sun, which, however, is to be clearly distinguished both from the eye—though the eye is, of all our organs, the most like the sun—and from the eye's faculty, sight. In fact the eye derives its faculty 'as a sort of effluence dispensed by the sun'. And as a result of this effluence the eye is enabled to see, among other things, the Sun itself.

The passage summarized in this last paragraph runs, again in a full and literal translation, as follows:

Have you ever noticed, I asked, how the creator of the senses made the faculty of seeing and being seen much the most extravagant sense?

No, not really, he said.

Then look at it this way. Is there anything extra of another kind required before hearing can hear or a sound be heard, in the absence of which third factor hearing will not hear nor the sound be heard?

No, nothing, he said.

I fancy, said I, that there are not many senses—indeed I might almost say there are none—that require anything extra of this kind. Or can you mention any?

No, I can't, he said.

But don't you see that sight and its object require this extra thing?

How?

When sight is in a man's eyes and its possessor tries to use it, and when colour is in its objects, still unless there is also present a third kind of thing, which exists specially for this purpose, sight, you know, will see nothing and the colours will remain unseen.

What do you mean by this thing? he asked.

What you call light, I answered.

Quite true, he said.

So the sense of sight and the faculty of being seen are united by a bond that is in no small way more valuable than other links—unless indeed light is valueless.

It's far from being that, he said.

Then which of the gods in heaven would you credit as the author of light? Or whose light is it that causes our sight to see in the most lovely way and makes its objects visible?

The same god as you or anyone else would credit, he said; your question obviously refers to the sun.

Then does sight stand to this god like this?

How?

The sun is neither sight itself nor that in which sight is implanted—namely the eye.

No indeed.

But I fancy that the eye is most sun-like of all the sense organs.

Yes, much.

Then has it got the faculty it has as a sort of effluence dispensed by the sun?

Certainly.

Then while not itself sight, is the sun, as the cause of sight, itself seen by it?

Quite right, he said.

So far in the analogy Plato has been concerned exclusively with the visible, not the intelligible world. So far we have merely been presented with the only four relevant factors in the visible world; first the sun, second its light, third the eye and fourth its sight. And we have already been given three facts concerning the relation of the sun to the other three factors, with a fourth fact to be added later. We have been told, first, that the sun is not itself the same as either sight or the eye. Second, we have been told that the eye is, however, the most like the sun of all our organs and actually derives its power therefrom. We have been told, third, that as the cause of sight the sun makes visible not only other things but itself as well. And we shall soon be told, fourth, that the sun is not only the cause of the visibility of other things, it is also the cause of their generation, growth and nourishment—though no more, Plato adds, to be identified with generation than with sight.

So much for the visible world; for though a few minor details are yet to be added, the rest of the analogy, from 508 b 12 to 509 c 4, is mainly concerned with the application to the intelligible world. Accordingly we are next given the four necessary equations. The sun stands for the Idea of the Good, sight for intelligence, the eye for the soul (this is implied rather than explicit in the clear parallel between the soul at 508 d 4 and the eyes at 508 c 4) and light stands for the truth. Just as, therefore, the sun is the source of light, so the Idea of the Good is the source of truth. And so, *mutatis mutandis,* we arrive at the corresponding four facts as follows. The Idea of the Good itself is not to be identified either with knowledge or with the mind. Truth and knowledge are, however, the most akin of all things to the Idea of the Good. As the cause of knowledge the Idea of the Good makes intelligible not only all the other Ideas but itself as well. And the Idea of the Good is not only the cause of the intelligibility of the other Ideas, it is also the cause of their very being—though no more to be identified with being than with knowledge. So, just as the eye sees clearly in daylight but blinks helplessly in darkness, the soul understands clearly in the light of truth which shines from the Idea of the Good, but has only shifting opinion about 'that which is mixed with darkness, that which comes into being and perishes'. And so again, several pages later (518e), Plato adds that, just as you cannot put sight into a man but only turn his eyes to the light, likewise 'the virtue of wisdom', unlike other virtues, cannot be implanted, and for the matter of that, being more godlike, it cannot lose its power either; it can only be converted from mischief to good.

The passage in which Plato tells us all this, in a different order from that in which, for the sake of clarity, I have just summarized it, runs literally as follows:

Such then, said I, you may say is my account of the offspring of the Good, that which the Good engendered to be analogous to itself; what the Good is in the intelligible sphere, in its relation to intelligence and its objects, its offspring is in the visible sphere, in its relation to sight and the objects of sight.

How? he asked. Do explain more fully.

You know, I replied, that our eyes, when they are no longer turned towards objects which are lit by daylight but only by starlight, seem dim and almost blind, as if they contained no pure sight.

Certainly.

But when the sun is shining, those same eyes, I fancy, see clearly and it is plain that they do contain sight.

Yes indeed.

Then consider the case of the soul in the same way. When it is fixed on a region where truth and reality are shining, it understands and knows and plainly contains intelligence. But when it is turned towards that which is mixed with darkness, that which comes into being and perishes, then it grows dim and has only beliefs which shift here and there, and seems like something without intelligence.

Yes, it does.

Then that which imparts truth to the objects of knowledge, and gives the power of knowing to him who knows, you should affirm to be the Idea of the Good. It is the cause of knowledge and truth, and you should think of it as being known. But while knowledge and truth are both beautiful you would be right in thinking that it is different and yet more beautiful than either. Just as in that other world it's right to think of light and sight as sun-like but wrong to identify them with the sun, so here too it's right to think both knowledge and truth like the Good but wrong to identify either of them with it. The standing of the Good is to be yet more highly revered.

You are talking of an inconceivable beauty, he said, if it imparts knowledge and truth, yet itself excels them in beauty. Surely you cannot mean that it is pleasure.

Hush! I said, I'd like you rather to consider the analogy a stage further.

How?

I fancy you'd agree that the sun imparts to the objects of sight, not only the power of being seen, but also their generation, growth and nourishment—not however being itself generation.

Of course not.

Then you must agree also that not only their knowability comes to the objects of knowledge from the Good, but also their being and reality comes to them from the same source—although the Good is not itself being but lies yet beyond being and transcends it in dignity and power.

Glaucon replied very comically, Apollo! What an astonishing transcendence.

It's your fault, I said; you made me tell you what I think about it.

That brings us to the end of the analogy of the Sun, and but for the fact that it is almost immediately followed by the further analogy of the Divided Line there would be little more to be said. Despite the wealth of its new content the whole passage is essentially simple enough. Its general purpose is at any rate clear at first sight, namely to assert, allegorically rather than literally, the relation of the Idea of the Good, which 'lies yet beyond being', both to the other Ideas and to the mind, or intelligence, which seeks to apprehend it. That purpose demands that Plato concern himself only with the sense of sight and its objects. Once sight has been singled out, in the prefatory section, from all the other senses, the introduction of any other sense than sight would serve only to confuse and thwart the whole purpose of the analogy. And so we find that Plato speaks only of 'sight', and of either 'the visible' or 'the objects of sight', never, once sight has been distinguished, of 'perception' or 'the perceptible', still less of 'opinion' or 'the objects of opinion'. There can be no question in the analogy of the Sun, as there certainly is in that of the Divided Line, whether or not sight is intended to represent all forms of fallible perception or opinion. Sight, so far, simply symbolizes knowledge; to interpret it in any wider sense is, again so far, to destroy the whole analogy. There is, in a word, no place yet either for any of the senses except sight or for opinion, whether right or wrong. If we remember the four relevant factors in the visible world, and those four only, we shall remember all that Plato is here trying to teach us of the nature and constitution of the intelligible world. Reduced to the barest bones it amounts to this. The sun in the visible world is analogous to the Idea of the Good in the intelligible;

each is supreme in its proper sphere. As the sun gives light, so the Idea of the Good gives truth; and as the eye cannot see except in daylight, so the mind or intelligence cannot understand except in the light of truth which shines from the Idea of the Good. The eye therefore represents the intelligence; and just as the eye is the most akin of our organs to the sun, so is the intelligence to the Idea of the Good. But at the same time, just as the sun is not itself to be identified with either the eye or its sight, so the Idea of the Good is not to be identified with either the intelligence or its understanding. Rather, just as the sun makes visible not only all other things but itself as well, so the Idea of the Good makes intelligible not only all the other Ideas but also itself. And finally, just as the sun is the cause, not only of the visibility of other things, but also of their birth and growth, so the Idea of the Good is the cause, not only of the intelligibility of the other Ideas, but of their very being. So much at least we learn for the first time from the analogy of the Sun. It is a great deal, but there is even more to come.

Seven lines of Greek intervene between the end of the analogy of the Sun and the beginning of that of the Divided Line. Those seven lines have received less attention than they deserve; they are vital to a correct interpretation of the analogy that follows. Here they are, beginning exactly where the last excerpt left off (509 c 5):

Don't stop at any price, he said, or at least go on explaining the simile of the sun, if there is anything at all to be added.

There is a great deal to be added, I replied.

Then don't omit the least bit of it, he said.

I fancy, I said, that I shall omit a lot; but for all that I won't deliberately omit anything that can be said at this moment.

No, don't.

The analogy of the Sun, as I have said, is essentially straightforward. Sight is singled out from the other senses and its relation both to the sun and to light explained. The sensible world, therefore, which for the moment, and for Plato exceptionally, is being regarded as analogous to the intelligible, is called always 'visible', never either 'sensible' or (to borrow a word from Adam) 'opinable'. These seven transitional lines should be considered with that in mind. Glaucon, in so many words, presses Socrates to 'go on explaining the simile of the sun' and Socrates consents to the request. In other words —and the point is so obvious that it seems to be constantly overlooked—the Divided Line analogy is explicitly introduced as a continuation of the analogy of the Sun.

We ought surely to expect, therefore, that as in the analogy of the Sun, so again in that of the Divided Line, the sensible world will be represented by the solitary sense of sight and its objects. That at any rate is precisely what we find. In the two sentences with which Socrates is made to introduce the Divided Line, he speaks of the sensible world only—but that twice—as 'visible';[1] and he virtually underlines his use of the word by a gratuitous and not very funny etymological joke about the fanciful derivation of the Greek word for 'heaven' from the word for 'to see'. And again in his next short speech he

[1] ὁρατόν.

uses only, but again he uses twice, the alternative form, 'that which is seen'.[1] There is only one point in the whole passage at which our expectation is belied, at the end of Socrates' next speech but one. There, certainly, the word which Adam translated 'opinable' does suddenly take the place of the usual 'visible'. That solitary exception, however, permits of a ready explanation, which will be given in due course. Otherwise our expectation is amply fulfilled. Plato seems to have gone out of his way, in the introductory section of the Divided Line, to have included one or other of the two words meaning 'visible' wherever he possibly could.

This short transitional passage, which seems to link the analogy of the Divided Line so clearly and closely to that of the Sun, might still of course be dismissed as nothing but an artificial device of style designed to secure a natural continuity. But that escape too is easily blocked. The Divided Line starts with a résumé of the conclusions of the Sun. The two worlds of the Sun analogy, and their respective Kings, provide Plato with the material on which he is to work in the Divided Line. That is the strongest of all supports for the contention that the Divided Line, not only for stylistic reasons but genuinely, is to be taken as a continuation of the Sun. Indeed, so far as I can see, there is no possible escape from that conclusion; whence it follows that the orthodox interpretation of the Divided Line, as it is admirably presented, for instance, by Adam in his edition of the *Republic*, has already been undermined. For whereas I believe that the Divided Line,

[1] ὁρώμενον.

just like the Sun before it, aims to throw light on the contents of the intelligible world by means of the analogy with the visible, the orthodox view maintains that it aims to do what nobody has ever suspected the Sun of doing, namely to give us a complete hierarchical classification of the contents of both worlds alike, the visible as well as the intelligible.

One of Plato's more baffling tendencies is to condense his writing in proportion as his thought becomes more profound. That particular tendency is especially pronounced throughout the whole of the Divided Line. The difficulty of the Divided Line consists largely in the fact that on several occasions Plato omits to tell us what he could quite easily have told us in two or three words and what, if he had seen fit to tell us, would have solved our main problems. Why should he have teased us with these apparent sins of omission? Was it because he considered what he omitted to be irrelevant, or did he leave it to his readers' imaginations to fill the gaps? On the answer to that question will depend our whole interpretation of the Divided Line; or in other words, a correct interpretation must depend on a correct reading of Plato's psychology. Our only reliable clues to Plato's psychology are to be found in Plato's own words; and since there is no other passage in the whole of his writings that bears any real resemblance to the Divided Line, that amounts to saying Plato's own words in this single condensed passage. At this stage, therefore, not only what Plato says, but almost equally what he omits to say, assumes a special importance.

The directions which Plato gives us for drawing and

dividing the line admirably illustrate his temporary terseness. We are told to draw a line, which we will call *AB*,
and to divide it unequally at a point *C* so that *AC* is
longer than *CB*. Then again we have to divide both segments at points *D* and *E* in such a way that *BD* is to *DC* as
CE is to *EA* as *BC* is to *CA*. The line is drawn hori-
zontally in most editions, presumably for the printer's convenience, but it should certainly be drawn
vertically for the simple reason that what it represents is a vertical scale of reality. It is divided,
Plato tells us, in proportions which symbolize
'comparative clearness or obscurity'; the shorter
the segment, in other words, the more obscure its
contents. Incidentally, if we carry out the instructions, *DC* is bound to equal *CE*, and that fact has
been used by at least one commentator for the
most improbable purposes; as Plato's failure to
mention the fact strongly suggests, it is an unfortunate
and irrelevant accident. Although it is a geometrical
impossibility at once to preserve the proportions, which
are all-important, and to make each segment longer than
the one below it, that is what Plato, had it been possible,
would have wished to do.

So much for the diagram itself; Plato proceeds at once
to its significance. We are told first that the two major
divisions, *BC* and *CA*, represent respectively the two
worlds of the Sun analogy, *BC* the visible world and *CA*
the intelligible. And thereupon we start on the minor
segments, beginning with the bottom segment, *BD*, and
working steadily upwards. And if at this stage I quote the

A
E
C
D
B

passage into which Plato compresses, not only all that I have so far written about the Divided Line, but also his description of the contents of the segment *BD*, his temporary terseness will be immediately apparent.

Please realise, then, I went on, that as we were saying, there are these two, the Sun and the Idea of the Good, of which the latter reigns over the intelligible class or realm, the former over the visible; I don't say 'over heaven' for fear that you think I'm punning. Anyhow, have you grasped these two classes,[1] visible and intelligible?

Yes, I have.

Then take a line divided into two unequal segments and divide each segment again in the same proportion. One segment stands for the visible class, the other for the intelligible. You will see the comparative clearness or obscurity of the segments. In the visible sphere one segment consists of images; and by images I mean first shadows, then reflections in water or in any compact, smooth and polished surface, and everything of that kind, if you see what I mean.

Yes, I do.

That is the sum total of what Plato sees fit to tell his readers about the contents of the segment *BD*. It consists of visual images—shadows and reflections and 'everything of that kind'. Many scholars follow Adam in maintaining that these last four words show that Plato's 'shadows and reflections' are intended to exemplify the whole category of second-hand impressions and opinions. But there are three arguments which together seem fatal to such a view. In the first place the Divided Line is, as we saw, explicitly introduced as a continuation of the

[1] This is a good instance of Plato's use of the word εἶδος in the sense of 'class' or 'kind'.

Sun, where no such exemplification can conceivably be intended. Secondly, the whole lower segment, *BC*, is twice in the same sentence called 'visible' rather than 'sensible' or 'opinable'. And thirdly, the actual examples of his 'images' which Plato condescends to give us are undeniably and exclusively visual. When we come to the allegory of the Cave and consider the condition of the prisoners in it, we shall there find Plato representing them as not only seeing shadows but as also hearing echoes and, which is even more important, as holding opinions about both. In the allegory of the Cave, therefore, we are left in no doubt at all that Plato does indeed mean the whole category of second-hand impressions. But if he means the same here, then why does he not here too add the words 'and echoes also'? He easily could have done so in two words, whether with or instead of 'everything of that kind'. The latter part of this third argument is admittedly negative, but it too, like the positive arguments, very strongly suggests that Plato is still distinguishing sight both from all the other senses and from opinion. Indeed, if this is not so, then Plato can fairly be accused of having deliberately misled us. And moreover there is one last reason why Plato should still be singling out sight from the rest of the senses, namely that a visual reflection is at once so like the original as to be sometimes indistinguishable from it and yet really wholly different because it is in a different medium and usually also in different dimensions.

Plato's description of the contents of the next minor segment, *DC*, affords the strongest confirmation of these arguments. This time we are vouchsafed a mere two lines

A⌐
E⊦

C⊦

D⊦

B⌐

of Greek, which follow immediately on the end of the last excerpt (510 a 5–6). They run thus:

> Then take the second segment to stand for what the first resembles, the living things around us and the whole class of natural or manufactured things.
>
> All right, he said.

This passage is so brief and straightforward that it permits of little discussion. In this instance it would have been even easier for Plato, had he so wished, to broaden the scope of his examples; yet he still confines himself rigidly to the objects of sight. Once again, if he really wished us to include in this segment the whole realm of sense-perception and opinion, he has for some unimaginable reason deliberately deceived us.

That is all that we are told about the two lower segments individually, but now comes a short paragraph on the relation between the two. And this is the decisive paragraph since it is here that, in place of one or other of the two words meaning 'visible', we suddenly find instead the word meaning 'opinable', without which the significance of the whole passage could hardly have been in dispute. This is how it runs:

> Would you also, I asked, be willing to admit that the line has been so divided, with regard to truth and falsehood, that as the object of opinion stands to that of knowledge, so stands the copy to the original?
>
> Yes, he said, I'm quite willing.

On this one short passage, if not indeed on the one word meaning 'the object of opinion', the whole orthodox interpretation is based. The segment *BC* is here unques-

tionably described as 'the object of opinion'; and moreover 'the object of opinion', as opposed to that of knowledge, has equally unquestionably been defined earlier
(v, 479 d 3) as 'the many conventional views of the masses
on beauty and other such things'. It follows, argues Adam,
that *BC* must contain 'not only visibles but other opin-
ables as well' and is intended to present a complete classification of the contents of the sensible world. Once again,
therefore, we shall have to analyse this sentence, if not
word by word, at least phrase by phrase.

The solitary datum rests in the concluding clause of
Socrates' speech, 'so stands the copy to the original'.
Since a copy is often just as clear as the original and may
even be indistinguishable from it, the appropriate distinction between a copy and its original is not a distinction of
clarity but one of authenticity. The appropriate phrase for
Plato to use in the present context is not, therefore, the
phrase which he used a little earlier (509 d 9), 'clarity and
obscurity', but rather the phrase which he actually does
use, 'truth and falsehood'. So much is obvious. And the
rest of the argument seems to follow inevitably. For
throughout the whole of the analogy of the Sun, and
throughout the whole of Plato's condensed account of
the lower main division of the Line, the visible world is
for once not being opposed to the intelligible as the spurious is opposed to the genuine: it is being regarded for
the time being as analogous. The contrast, therefore,
between the object of opinion and that of knowledge becomes suddenly quite inappropriate at the moment when
Plato wishes to express the relation between a copy and

A
E
C
D
B

its original. The obvious if not indeed the only word to oppose to 'the object of knowledge' in this new context is the word which Plato actually uses. The introduction of the new metaphor of copy and original has eventually forced upon Plato a temporary change in his vocabulary. The contrast between clarity and obscurity, which was the appropriate contrast so long as Plato was distinguishing between objects in sunlight and objects in darkness, has to give place, when the time comes to define the relation of the segment DC to BD, to the contrast between truth and falsehood; and that in turn involves the temporary abandonment of the recent analogy between the visible and the intelligible in favour of the earlier contrast between the objects of opinion and those of knowledge. But until this change becomes unavoidable, Plato's language throughout the whole passage so far considered suggests as strongly as could be that his main concern is still with the analogy between visible and intelligible.

The conclusion to which this detailed discussion leads should be obvious enough. I believe that the purpose of the Divided Line, as a continuation of the analogy of the Sun, is to use sight and the two classes of visible things to illustrate intelligence and the two classes of intelligible things. In that case, of course, the segment BC is no more intended to give us any kind of classification than is the visible world in the Sun analogy. Both Sun and Divided Line are illustrative rather than classificatory. In the analogy of the Sun four relevant factors in the visible world, and four only, are used to illustrate the relations subsisting between the four analogous factors in the intelligible world. But the Sun analogy, apart from calling the sun itself 'King' of the visible sphere, was not in the least concerned to draw distinctions of status between the various objects of sight. The Divided Line is therefore complementary to the Sun. In the Divided Line the two relevant classes of things in the visible world, actual objects and their shadows or reflections, are used to illustrate the relations subsisting between the two analogous classes in the intelligible world. The primary purpose of the whole upper division of the Line, CA, is naturally to tell us what is the nature of these two classes of the intelligible things. The whole lower division, BC, being purely illustrative, is included only for the sake of the upper. But it is clearly essential to a right understanding of the upper division to decide first exactly what relation Plato is meaning to describe between the two segments of the lower division.

Even before reading what Plato has to say about the upper division, we have then one datum. The proportions of the Line indicate that the entities in the segment CE stand to those in EA as the reflections in BD stand to their originals in DC. The relation between the two classes in the intelligible world is, in other words, analogous to the relation between visible shadows or reflections and the objects which cast them. Plato himself at once gives us a summary of the essential distinction between the two upper segments, CE and EA. This is what he says, again following immediately after the last excerpt (510b2):

Now then see how the intelligible division is to be divided. How?

A ⊤
E ⊦
C ⊦
D ⊦
B ⊥

Like this. In one segment the soul uses as images the objects which, in the lower division, were themselves reproduced, and is forced to use hypotheses in its enquiry; it isn't moving towards a first principle but towards a conclusion. But in the other segment it moves from a hypothesis towards a first principle which is no mere hypothesis; without the use of the images involved in the lower segment, it conducts its investigation in terms of Ideas themselves and Ideas alone.

Once again Plato has contrived to pack the most substantial contents into a disproportionately small container. Still working upwards, he tells us first two facts about the segment *CE*. In that segment the soul uses as 'images' the objects in *DC* which were themselves reflected in *BD*. The word for 'images', incidentally, is the same as that used in the description of the contents of *BD*. This is an important point because it makes the relation of each segment to that immediately above it uniform throughout the whole Line. *BD* contains images of *DC*, the objects in *DC* are images of the contents of *CE* and *CE* contains images of *EA*. That is a neat feature of the analogy. And at the same time, Plato adds, the soul moves in *CE* from a hypothesis, not upwards towards a first principle, but downwards to a conclusion. Then we are given the corresponding two facts about *EA*: that here the soul makes no use of images but is concerned solely with the Ideas; and that this time it moves from a hypothesis upwards to a first principle which is not a hypothesis at all.

Plato himself clearly felt that this particular paragraph was excessively condensed, for he immediately makes Glaucon evince the natural reaction:

'I don't altogether understand what you are saying.'
So Socrates proceeds to expand the two facts already given
about *CE*, the second fact in his first speech, the first in his
second. The passage continues without a break as follows:

Then I'll say it again, I went on; you'll understand more
easily after what has been said already. I imagine you know
that those whose business is with geometry and calculation
and the like take as hypotheses the odd and the even, geometrical figures, three kinds of angle and so forth in each
branch of study. They treat them as hypotheses and carry on
as if they knew them; they don't bother to give an account of
them, to themselves or to anybody else, on the ground that
they are clear to all. Beginning from these they proceed step
by step, until they eventually arrive self-consistently at whatever it was that they embarked on their enquiry to establish.

Yes, I certainly know that, he said.

Then you know, too, that they use visible figures[1] and
conduct their discussions about them, while not really thinking about them at all but about the things which these figures
reproduce; they are really concerned with the square itself,
the diagonal itself (rather than the diagonal they draw) and
so on. These actual models or diagrams, which themselves
cast shadows or are imaged in water, they use in turn as
images, while they seek to see the actual realities which can
only be seen by abstraction.[2]

Quite true, he said.

---

[1] Again the word εἴδη, in another of its non-technical senses.

[2] The word rendered 'abstraction' is διάνοια, a key word in the rest
of Part III. Admittedly 'abstraction' is normally a process rather than a
state of mind; but even so it seems, in the context of *Republic* VI-VII,
to convey more of the sense of διάνοια than any other single English
word. A possible alternative is 'insight', which is at least intermediate
in status between comprehension or reason and belief or opinion (see
p. 163). Other renderings which are in themselves attractive, such as
'reasoning' or 'perception', fail to satisfy this essential requirement.

A
E
C
D
B

Socrates' expansion in this passage of the same two facts about *CE* involves particularisation; he is here concerned only with students of the various branches of mathematics. Plato is once again using mathematical method to illustrate a metaphysical theory. The mathematicians' hypotheses, he tells us, are 'the odd and the even, figures and the three kinds of angle'. These things are 'hypotheses', or assumptions, because they are simply taken for granted. No attempt is made to give an account of them by deriving them from something more ultimate, but instead mathematicians proceed to argue downwards from them, by a series of self-consistent steps, until they arrive at the conclusions which they set out to establish. And at the same time mathematicians use diagrams in two dimensions or models in three as images or reflections of a truer class of entities. They draw a circle, for instance, and apparently discuss the drawing while thinking all the time of the original. And Plato's language, 'the square itself',[1] should leave no doubt that the original in question is the Idea of the Square. As Plato puts it literally, it is 'for the sake of the Idea of the Square' that a mathematician conducts his enquiry.

Such then are the same two facts about *CE* expressed in terms of mathematical procedure; and so much importance, evidently, does Plato attach to these two facts that he gives them to us for yet a third time in Socrates' next speech, which is in the nature of a final summary of this particular segment (511 a 3):

This then is the class[2] of things I spoke of as intelligible; but I said that the soul is forced to use hypotheses in its investigation

---

[1] τοῦ τετραγώνου αὐτοῦ.   [2] Again εἶδος.

of it, and does not proceed towards a first principle because it is unable to climb above its hypotheses. It uses as images those same objects that were reflected lower down, which were themselves regarded with respect as distinct in comparison with their reflections.

I gather, he said, that you're speaking of the subject-matter of geometry and related arts.

That concludes Plato's own account of the segment *CE*. The orthodox interpretation of the significance of the passage is based on frequent references in Aristotle to what he calls either 'the objects of mathematics' or 'the intermediates'.[1] A typical passage is *Metaphysics* A 987 b 14: 'Again, in addition to Ideas and sensible things, he [Plato] says that there exists an intermediate class in the objects of mathematics, which differ from sensible things in being eternal and immutable and from Ideas in that, whereas each Idea is unique, there are many similar objects of mathematics.' These 'objects of mathematics', says the orthodox view, which can be exemplified by the two twos in the equation $2+2=4$ or by two congruent triangles, are exactly what is required in the segment *CE*. The Divided Line itself shows them to be intermediate between the Ideas in *EA* and the particulars in *DC*, and Plato's language in describing the mathematical procedure adopted in *CE* is precisely apposite to the doctrine of intermediates. The orthodox interpretation concludes, therefore, that Plato had already by the time he wrote the *Republic* recognized the existence of the class of mathematical intermediates; that he intended us to place them

[1] τὰ μαθηματικά or τὰ μεταξύ.

^A in the intermediate segment, *CE*; and that he therefore
^E goes on, at 511 d 4, to attribute to them the special faculty
of 'abstraction'¹ as being, in his own words, 'something
^C in between opinion and intelligence'.

^D   This interpretation, a full statement of which can be
^B found in the Appendix to Book VII of Adam's edition, is
largely irresistible. The only question is whether it goes
far enough. Granted that the objects of mathematics are
unquestionably to be included in *CE*, the question remains whether that is all that we are meant to include
there. The key to the problem is to be found, I believe, in
the phrase 'the square itself', which, by Adam's interpretation, must mean, not the Idea, but the mathematical
intermediate, 'the square by itself', as he puts it, 'i.e. apart
from its embodiment in perceivable squares'. But we
must surely do Plato the justice of assuming that, in as
important and condensed a passage as this, he is at least
using every word with careful thought. And in that case
we surely ought not too readily to conclude that when he
wished to speak of the mathematical intermediates as
deliberately opposed to the Ideas he could have used the
very phrase by which he habitually described the Ideas
themselves; especially when, by the simple expedient of
substituting the plural 'squares themselves' for the singular 'the square itself', he could not only have avoided any
possibility of misunderstanding but at the same time have
underlined the doctrine of mathematical intermediates.
Incidentally, Adam himself is reduced to rationalizing the
singular here as generic, which at least shows that he was

¹ Again διάνοια.

156

aware of the difficulty. Plato's language, which must remain the decisive consideration, seems in fact to suggest as strongly as it could that his point about the geometrician's thought is this: that, originally stimulated by visible diagrams or models, it ranges upwards, not only as far as the intermediates, but to the Ideas themselves. It does not, however, go on to give an account of these Ideas; it simply takes them for granted, or, as Plato would put it, 'hypothesizes' them.

Having got thus far, we are inevitably reminded of the *Phaedo*, which presented us for the first time with the two different movements of thought, the upward movement and the downward movement. The downward movement, by hypothesizing a plurality of as yet unco-ordinated Ideas, proceeded to give an account of the particulars of the sensible world. The upward movement, which perhaps first suggested itself to Plato just because he was dissatisfied with this plurality, worked upwards from precisely the same hypothesis to ever higher levels of reality in order to co-ordinate and so give an account of the Ideas themselves. In Plato's description of the segment *CE* of the Divided Line we have a more detailed account of the downward movement of thought. Indeed he expressly says that in *CE* the mind starts from a hypothesis, presumably the postulation of the plurality of unco-ordinated Ideas, and moves thence not to a first principle but to a conclusion. Mathematics do of course provide the ideal illustration of this procedure because, as Plato says, they do take for granted the material on which they work, such as magnitude and its various

properties, and they do employ an essentially deductive method. And possibly even, since we concluded that the lower division of the Line was not intended to contain a complete classification at all, we should rest content with the same conclusion about the upper division as well and include in *CE* only the objects of mathematical studies. But in that case we must at all costs remember that, according to the accounts in both the *Phaedo* and the *Republic*, mathematics are by no means unique in starting from the hypothesis of the Ideas and working downwards from there to particulars. Even Plato's own account in the *Phaedo* of why a thing is beautiful or large does exactly the same. It starts from the hypothesis of the Ideas of Beauty and Magnitude and then works downwards. And for the matter of that, mathematics do not appear to be unique either in possessing intermediates as objects; any formula or law, such as the formulae of chemistry or the laws of economics, seems to present entities of a similar status. Two extant fragments (96 and 98) from Empedocles' poem *On Nature*, with which Plato would certainly have been familiar, give us, for instance, his formulae for bone and for blood respectively. Bone is compounded of two 'parts'[1] of earth, two of water and four of fire, while blood consists of the four elements 'in almost equal proportions'. Clearly these 'parts' or 'proportions' are not Ideas, or they could not be multiplied as in the formula for bone; and clearly they are not particulars either, since the formula is independent of its particular embodiments. And so I conclude that Plato, even if in

[1] μερέων.

CE, as in *BD*, he did not intend an exhaustive classification, still cannot have regarded mathematics as unique but only as affording the most obvious and apposite examples of the significance of the segment *CE*. *CE* represents the downward movement of the *Phaedo*. First, it takes for granted as ultimate the plurality of unco-ordinated Ideas and so gives no account of them. And second, working by deduction from that hypothesis, it is thereby enabled to give an account of the particulars of the sensible world.

We would seem to be justified, therefore, in placing at the point *E*, or perhaps rather in aligning on a horizontal line through the point *E*, the plurality of unco-ordinated Ideas; Man and Pig, Bed and Shuttle, Piety and Justice, Magnitude and Equality, and countless others, arranged as yet in no sort of order or classification among themselves. *CE* in fact stretches, as we would expect, from the particulars of *DC*, through the intermediates, to the plurality of Ideas at *E*. 'But supposing', as Plato put it very briefly in the *Phaedo*, 'that someone fastened on to your hypothesis and you had to give an account of the hypothesis itself . . . you would do so by hypothesizing another hypothesis that seemed best of those above until you came to something adequate.' So the *Phaedo*, having discussed the downward movement of thought at comparative length, very briefly suggested the upward. And so again the Divided Line, having in *CE* described the downward movement, passes in *EA* to the upward. Already in the description of *CE* we have been told, by way of contrast, two facts about *EA*. In *EA*, as in *CE*, the mind

again starts from a hypothesis but this time works, not
downwards to a conclusion, but upwards 'towards a first
principle which is no mere hypothesis'; and this time too
it makes no use of the images which it used in *CE* but
'conducts its investigation in terms of Ideas themselves
and Ideas alone'. And when Plato turns to the segment
EA itself, as he now does without a break, this is how he
continues (511b3):

A, *E*, *C*, *D*, *B* [bracket labels in left margin]

Then by the other segment of the intelligible class you must
take me to mean that which the reason itself grasps by its
power of dialectic. Now it no longer regards its hypotheses as
first principles but as literally 'hypotheses', laid down like
stairs or spring-boards, from which it may climb as far as that
which is no longer hypothetical and come to the first principle
of everything. Grasping this, and clinging throughout to the
things which themselves cling to it, the reason will so descend
to its conclusion, never in any circumstances resorting to anything sensible, but using only the Ideas, in and by themselves,
and ending with the Ideas.

In this passage, alongside the same two facts which we
have already learnt, a third fact is added which is of vital
importance. Here we are not only told once again both
that in the segment *EA* the mind starts from a hypothesis,
whence it works upwards to a secure first principle, and
that it is now independent of the senses and concerned
exclusively with Ideas; we are told also that, having
climbed to the top of the staircase, it descends again step
by step to the bottom, which itself, however, lies still
within the realm of the Ideas. This of course, if read
without any introduction, would once again be exces-

sively condensed and obscure; but after the foregoing discussions of the *Phaedo* and the *Symposium*, the analogy of the Sun and the lowest three segments of the Divided Line, its general purport should be tolerably clear. The hypothesis from which, in *CE*, the mind proceeded to move downwards is exactly the same as that from which, in *EA*, it proceeds to climb upwards, the hypothesis of the plurality of unco-ordinated Ideas. Starting thence, the mind this time moves up through ever higher levels of reality until eventually it comes to the Idea of the Good itself, which proves to be the first principle of everything else and no longer a mere hypothesis but an absolute certainty.

Of the general nature of this upward pilgrimage we have already learnt a little from the *Phaedo* and the *Symposium*; but neither of those two dialogues, nor even the *Republic* itself, gives us any details of the successive steps which are to lead us up to the first principle of everything. For such details we have to await certain later dialogues, notably the *Phaedrus* and the *Sophist*. But though the details of the process still remain obscure, its consequences are at last plain. When it has eventually climbed up, as it were on a staircase, to the first principle of everything, then, as we have at last been told, the mind turns back again and begins to descend the selfsame stairs. 'Clinging to the things which themselves cling to the first principle', or, in other words, conscious throughout of their dependence on the Idea of the Good, the mind climbs down again as far as, but not a step further than, its starting-point in this segment, the plurality of unco-ordinated Ideas. But—and

A here we reach the point of vital importance in this fresh
development of the theory—its condition on its return is
E totally different from its condition when it embarked on
C the ascent. At the start the plurality of Ideas was a mere
D hypothesis of which no account had yet been or could yet
B be given; whereas now at last the Ideas are fully understood in their relation one to another, because they have
at last been co-ordinated in their dependence on the
non-hypothetical Idea of the Good. The very same things,
therefore, as in *CE* were simply taken for granted, 'the
Odd and the Even' and the rest, have now, by the discovery of their dependence on an ultimate principle,
become fully, and in the strict sense of the word, intelligible. That indeed is exactly what Glaucon says, among
other things, in the speech which immediately follows
and which virtually concludes the Divided Line; the
mathematicians' hypotheses or assumptions are, he says in
so many words, 'intelligible with the aid of a first
principle'. Here is the whole speech in which he says it:

I understand, he said; perhaps not completely, because you
seem to me to be describing an arduous undertaking. But
I see that you are wanting to distinguish that part of reality, or
the intelligible, which is the subject of the science of dialectic
as clearer than that which is the subject of the so-called arts.
For the latter, their hypotheses are their first principles; their
students are forced to study them by abstraction rather than
with the senses, but because in their investigation they don't
climb up to a first principle but work from hypotheses, you
don't think they exercise intelligence on their subject even
though it is intelligible with the aid of a first principle. And I
gather you call the state of mind of geometricians and the like

not intelligence but abstraction, as being something intermediate between intelligence and opinion.

You have taken my point very well, I said.

And there in my view, in spite of the fact that there are
still eight lines of Book VI to come, we reach the end of
the Divided Line. It tells us, probably, more of the kernel
of Platonism than any other passage yet cited. But at the
same time, as well as raising the various new problems discussed in this section, it serves to make two old problems
still more urgent. In the first place, how much besides
the moral and the mathematical Ideas is the ideal world
intended to contain? And second, what are the successive steps which lead us up to the eventual apprehension
of the Idea of the Good itself? Some light, even if not a
very clear light, is thrown on both these problems in the
remainder of the *Republic*.

The last eight lines of Book VI runs as follows:

Now then, take as corresponding to the four segments the
following four states of mind: attribute comprehension to the
highest segment, abstraction to the next, to the third belief
and to the last illusion.[1] Then arrange them proportionately,
regarding them as having the same degree of clarity as their
objects have of truth.

I understand, he said, and agree to arrange them as you
suggest.

[1] The *Concise Oxford Dictionary* defines each of these four terms in
(among others) exactly the sense here intended. Comprehension: 'act,
faculty, of understanding'. Abstraction: 'process of stripping an idea of
its concrete accompaniments'. Belief: 'acceptance as true or existing'.
Illusion: 'sensuous perception of an external object involving a false
belief'. The Greek words are νόησις, διάνοια, πίστις, εἰκασία, which
Cornford renders 'intelligence', 'thinking', 'belief', 'imagining'.

A And thereupon, with disastrously misleading effect, comes
the conventional division between Books VI and VII. If the
E division can be thought away, we can easily enough see how
C misleading it is. Admittedly at first glance these eight lines
D do look as if they belonged squarely to the Divided Line.
B But a closer inspection, which ignores the division between
the two Books, suggests that they belong equally squarely
to the allegory of the Cave. This is in fact another of those
transitional passages, just such as we met between the analogies of the Sun and the Divided Line, which are designed
to link one episode in a Platonic dialogue to the next.

The analogy of the Sun singled out sight from the
remainder of the senses and used it and its objects to
throw light on intelligence and the objects of intelligence.
Then came the Divided Line, as a continuation of the
Sun. The purpose of the Divided Line was to use the two
classes of visible things, physical objects and their shadows
or reflections, to throw light on the two classes of intelligible things, the Ideas as co-ordinated and understood
in their dependence on the Idea of the Good and the Ideas
as hypothetically postulated and unco-ordinated. And
now the Divided Line is itself to be followed by the Cave,
the purpose of which is wholly different. Unlike either
the Sun or the Divided Line, the Cave is to give us a
picture of every state of mind through which a man may
pass, from a state of total illusion to a state of total enlightenment. No longer are we concerned solely with
sight and its objects, as illustrating the nature and contents
of the intelligible world. We have passed from strictly
limited analogy to comprehensive allegory.

The transition is effected with remarkable speed and apparent ease in the eight lines just quoted. Having concluded the Divided Line with Glaucon's summary, Plato suddenly here suggests, as Adam would have us believe that he has been suggesting throughout the Divided Line, that the visible objects and their reflections in the lower division, *BC*, can after all, instead of being singled out, for the sake of the analogy, from the objects of all the other senses, be regarded henceforth as representative of the whole realm of opinion. He is here setting the stage for the next scene, and he accordingly resorts, exactly as he had at the beginning of the Divided Line, to a number of imperatives. The Divided Line required only two, 'realize' at 509 d 1 and 'divide' six lines lower down. The Cave needs no less than five, only the first three of which—'take', 'attribute' and 'arrange'—come in the passage just quoted. The remaining two—literally 'liken' and 'see'—come in the first two lines of Book VII. And incidentally Book VII opens with the words 'Then after this' or 'Next'—that is, 'When you have carried out the stage directions already given'—and then rapidly completes the same set of directions. Every indication points the same way. Had not the division between the two Books obscured the issue, these new directions, which set the stage for the Cave, would have run on without interruption and we should have seen without any difficulty that what Plato is really saying in this transitional passage can be paraphrased thus: 'The lower segments of the Line, the visible objects in *DC* and their reflections in *BD*, have now served their primary purpose of providing us with

A an analogy or illustration. With the aid of that analogy
we now understand the relation between the two classes
E in the ideal world. Now therefore, instead of singling
C sight out, as we have been doing throughout the analogies
D of the Sun and the Divided Line, from all the other senses,
B let us regard it instead as standing for the whole class of
second-hand impressions, not only of the senses but of the
judgment as well. Instead of confining *BD* to the seeing
of visible reflections, let us think of it henceforth as
representing the imagining of anything whatever that is
unreal; and instead of confining *DC* to the seeing of actual
concrete objects, let us now take it as standing for any
form of confident belief about anything which, through
its ceaselessly changing nature, does not admit of true
knowledge. Henceforth, in a word, in place of the recent
analogy between the visible and the intelligible, we are
reverting to the old contrast, emphasized at the end of
Book v, between the objects of opinion, or particulars,
and the objects of knowledge, or Ideas.'

The purpose of the Cave, then, is to tell us how, although we must originally be surrounded by the particular and incessantly changing objects of opinion, we
may yet struggle upward to the eventual apprehension of
the constant objects of knowledge. The Cave is thus a
passage of a different nature from either the Sun or the
Divided Line; a passage in which Plato is no longer concerned to express certain detailed and rather difficult relations between the various grades of reality which the
universe contains, but rather to paint, from a different
angle from that of the *Symposium*, an imaginative and all-

embracing picture of the pilgrimage of man. It can legitimately, therefore, be understood in the terms of poetry
as much as in those of philosophy; the two are once again
merged. And so instead of my own literal translation
I revert to the more readable and essentially faithful version of Cornford. This is how it runs, beginning from the
first word of Book VII:

Next, said I, here is a parable to illustrate the degrees in which
our nature may be enlightened or unenlightened. Imagine the
condition of men living in a sort of cavernous chamber under-
ground, with an entrance open to the light and a long passage
all down the cave. Here they have been from childhood,
chained by the leg and also by the neck, so that they cannot
move and can see only what is in front of them, because the
chains will not let them turn their heads. At some distance
higher up is the light of a fire burning behind them; and between the prisoners and the fire is a track with a parapet built
along it, like the screen at a puppet-show, which hides the
performers while they show their puppets over the top.

I see, said he.

Now behind this parapet imagine persons carrying along
various artificial objects, including figures of men and animals
in wood or stone or other materials, which project above the
parapet. Naturally, some of these persons will be talking,
others silent.

It is a strange picture, he said, and a strange sort of prisoners.

Like ourselves, I replied; for in the first place prisoners so
confined would have seen nothing of themselves or of one
another, except the shadows thrown by the fire-light on the
wall of the Cave facing them, would they?

Not if all their lives they had been prevented from moving
their heads.

And they would have seen as little of the objects carried past.

A
|
E— Of course.
| Now, if they could talk to one another, would they not
C— suppose that their words referred only to those passing shad-
| ows which they saw?
D— Necessarily.
| And suppose their prison had an echo from the wall facing
B— them? When one of the people crossing behind them spoke,
they could only suppose that the sound came from the shadow
passing before their eyes.

No doubt.

In every way, then, such prisoners would recognize as
reality nothing but the shadows of those artificial objects.

Inevitably.

Now consider what would happen if their release from the
chains and the healing of their unwisdom should come about
in this way. Suppose one of them set free and forced suddenly
to stand up, turn his head, and walk with eyes lifted to the
light; all these movements would be painful, and he would be
too dazzled to make out the objects whose shadows he had
been used to see. What do you think he would say, if someone told him that what he had formerly seen was meaningless
illusion, but now, being somewhat nearer to reality and turned
towards more real objects, he was getting a truer view? Suppose further that he were shown the various objects being
carried by and were made to say, in reply to questions, what
each of them was. Would he not be perplexed and believe the
objects now shown him to be not so real as what he formerly
saw?

Yes, not nearly so real.

And if he were forced to look at the fire-light itself, would
not his eyes ache, so that he would try to escape and turn back
to the things which he could see distinctly, convinced that they
really were clearer than these other objects now being shown
to him?

Yes.

And suppose someone were to drag him away forcibly up the steep and rugged ascent and not let him go until he had hauled him out into the sunlight, would he not suffer pain and vexation at such treatment, and, when he had come out into the light, find his eyes so full of its radiance that he could not see a single one of the things that he was now told were real?

Certainly he would not see them all at once.

He would need, then, to grow accustomed before he could see things in that upper world. At first it would be easiest to make out shadows, and then the images of men and things reflected in water, and later on the things themselves. After that, it would be easier to watch the heavenly bodies and the sky itself by night, looking at the light of the moon and stars rather than the Sun and the Sun's light in the day-time.

Yes, surely.

Last of all, he would be able to look at the Sun and contemplate its nature, not as it appears when reflected in water or any alien medium, but as it is in itself in its own domain.

No doubt.

And now he would begin to draw the conclusion that it is the Sun that produces the seasons and the course of the year and controls everything in the visible world, and moreover is in a way the cause of all that he and his companions used to see.

Clearly he would come at last to that conclusion.

Then if he called to mind his fellow prisoners and what passed for wisdom in his former dwelling-place, he would surely think himself happy in the change and be sorry for them. They may have had a practice of honouring and commending one another, with prizes for the man who had the keenest eye for the passing shadows and the best memory for the order in which they followed or accompanied one another, so that he could make a good guess as to which was going to come next. Would our released prisoner be likely to covet those prizes or to envy the men exalted to honour and power in the Cave?

A Would he not feel like Homer's Achilles, that he would far
sooner 'be on earth as a hired servant in the house of a land-
E less man' or endure anything rather than go back to his old
C beliefs and live in the old way?

Yes, he would prefer any fate to such a life.

D Now imagine what would happen if he went down again
B to take his former seat in the Cave. Coming suddenly out of
the sunlight, his eyes would be filled with darkness. He might
be required once more to deliver his opinion on those shadows,
in competition with the prisoners who had never been released,
while his eyesight was still dim and unsteady; and it might
take some time to become used to the darkness. They would
laugh at him and say that he had gone up only to come back
with his sight ruined; it was worth no one's while even to
attempt the ascent. If they could lay hands on the man who
was trying to set them free and lead them up, they would kill
him.[1]

Yes, they would.

This is the most famous of all Plato's allegories and its
general purport is plain enough. Although the prisoner's
progress from the moment of his release up to his ultimate contemplation of the sun itself is presented as continuous, it is still clearly divisible into four main stages,
distinguished one from the other by the degree of reality
of the objects at which he is looking.

First comes the stage of seeing only shadows and
hearing only echoes. When Socrates has completed his
description of this initial state, Glaucon remarks, not un-
naturally, 'It is a strange picture and a strange sort of
prisoners'; to which Socrates significantly replies 'Like

[1] As Cornford says here in a footnote, 'an allusion to the fate of
Socrates'.

ourselves'. He can only mean that this is the condition in which most of us spend most of our lives. That may seem obvious. But the reply carries with it an important consequence; for it shows yet again that the Cave and the Divided Line are not, as Adam thinks, precisely parallel the one to the other. This initial condition of the prisoner exactly corresponds, in Adam's view, to the lowest segment of the Line, *BD*. The segment *BD* contains visible shadows and reflections of visible objects, and even if, as is very doubtful, those visible reflections are meant to represent a much wider class of second-hand impressions, it is, even so, absurdly untrue to say, as Socrates is here made to say, that most of us spend most of our lives in seeing only reflections or hearing only echoes without ever seeing or hearing their originals. Socrates' brief remark, 'Like ourselves', affords therefore yet further confirmation of two important conclusions already reached. Not only are the Divided Line and the Cave not intended to be exactly parallel, but also the Cave gives us, what the Line does not, an exhaustive classification of the varying grades of reality in the world.

After the original condition of seeing only shadows, which does now indeed stand for having only second-hand opinions, comes the stage of looking at the actual objects which cast those shadows and at the fire which gives the necessary light. Here again it is important to note that these objects are themselves only, in Plato's own words, 'figures of men and animals in wood or stone or other materials'. They are only artificial copies of natural objects. Since the cave itself represents the visible

A
E
C
D
B

world in which we live, with the fire in the cave representing the actual sun, this second stage stands therefore for the relatively enlightened state of mind in which a man forms his own opinions about the objects and the actions of the sensible world. Only, however, relatively enlightened because, while it is clearly better to have first-hand than second-hand opinions, the objects and actions of the sensible world can admit only of opinion, never of knowledge. There is still a long way to go before the escaped prisoner begins to apprehend reality rather than its image.

Just as the cave in the allegory represents the sensible world, so the sensible world outside the cave represents the ideal world. And as in the Divided Line, so again in the allegory of the Cave, the contents of the ideal world are divided into two classes. One class, that which occupied the segment *CE* of the Divided Line, is represented in the Cave by 'shadows, and then the images of men and things reflected in water'. In the Divided Line the purpose of the whole lower division, *BC*, was purely illustrative: it was to present us with the relation of visible objects to their shadows or reflections. That was the relation which Plato wished us to apply to the upper division, *CA*. For that reason only, rather than for purposes of classification, was *BC* included at all. The present section of the Cave powerfully endorses these conclusions. For here again the relation between the two classes in the ideal world is presented in almost identical terms. The third stage of the prisoner's progress consists in the contemplation of the contents of the segment *CE*, the plurality of still unco-ordinated Ideas, which here, as in the Line, stand to the contents of *EA*, the Ideas as co-ordinated under the Good, as shadows and reflections stand to the objects which cast them.

The fourth and last stage, that of looking at the actual objects in the outside world, represents of course the gradual ascent, from hypothesis to higher hypothesis, which culminates in the contemplation of the Idea of the Good itself, represented in the allegory by the sun. The significant point here is that this single main stage consists of a series of minor stages: the escaped prisoner looks first at the sky by night and only gradually habituates his sight to an ever brighter light until at last he can endure to look at the sun itself. Plato is again suggesting that the ascent to the first principle is necessarily gradual. Not until the *Sophist* is this fact at all adequately explained, and by then the Idea of the Good has disappeared. But Books VI and VII of the *Republic* leave his intention in no doubt.

Just as, therefore, the Divided Line presents four sharply distinguished segments, so the Cave presents four distinct stages in the prisoner's progress. Hence the natural temptation to conclude that, in spite of certain minor inconsistencies attributable to the recalcitrance of allegorical material, the two passages are intended to be precisely parallel one to the other. Since I remain convinced, for the reasons already stressed, that such an interpretation is a misleading over-simplification, I will summarize what I believe to be the true relation between the three great analogies or allegories.

The purpose of the analogy of the Sun was very restricted. Beginning from the distinction between the

A
E
C
D
B

two worlds, the visible and the intelligible, but without attempting to distinguish between different classes of objects in either world, it first singled out from the visible world the only four relevant factors and then used them to throw light on the four analogous factors in the intelligible world. Next came the Divided Line, which, as an avowed continuation of the Sun, was designed to repair some at least of the Sun's deliberate omissions. Beginning from the same distinction between the two worlds, the Divided Line first showed that sight can look either at shadows and reflections or else at the actual objects which throw them, and then used the relation of images to originals to illuminate the relations between the two analogous classes of reality in the intelligible world. Neither the Sun nor the Divided Line purports to give an exhaustive and all-embracing picture. The Sun, asserting simply that what the sun is in the visible word, that the Idea of the Good is in the intelligible, gives a deliberately partial picture of each of the two worlds. The Divided Line, asserting simply that what reflections are to their originals, that the contents of the segment *CE* are to the contents of *EA*, gives perhaps a comprehensive picture of the intelligible world—though in that case the picture still lacks a great deal of detail—but a still deliberately partial picture of the visible world. So we come finally to the Cave; and the Cave begins with a reminder that sight and its objects, although recently singled out from the rest of the senses and temporarily regarded as analogous to knowledge, can equally be regarded as representative not only of all the other senses but of opinion as well, and so contrasted with knowledge. And thereafter, by this slight but dexterous switch, the Cave is at last enabled to give us an all-embracing picture. The four stages in the Cave, unlike the four segments in the Divided Line, cover every conceivable state of mind. Plato here gives us again, what he had given us before, from a different angle, in the *Symposium* but what he had not attempted to give in either Sun or Divided Line, a picture of the pilgrimage of the soul from total illusion to total enlightenment. A careful comparison of the two pictures, those of the *Symposium* and of the *Republic* respectively, is instructive and significant. The picture of the *Symposium* is liable to leave the impression that progress is automatic: once you have your foot on the bottom rung of the ladder you can hardly fail to climb to the top. The picture of the *Republic*, by the stress it lays on the pain caused by the increasing brightness of the light and on the prisoner's constant desire to return to the darkness whence he came, effectually counteracts that mistaken impression. For the picture of the *Republic*, unlike that of the *Symposium*, is only a preliminary to certain practical proposals. The three great allegories of *Republic* VI and VII are not three related but independent wholes, like the three pictures of a triptych; they are rather the three complementary and interdependent parts of a single whole, like the three legs of a tripod. Together they construct the metaphysical basis of Plato's theory and syllabus of higher education.

Plato's theory of education, which springs directly and naturally out of the allegory of the Cave, is based on the

A

E

C

D

B

belief, already discernible in the theory of 'recollection' in the *Meno*, that knowledge is not acquired but innate. The crucial passage on this topic begins at 518b6, little more than a page after the end of the Cave, and runs, in Cornford's version, as follows:

If this is true, then, we must conclude that education is not what it is said to be by some, who profess to put knowledge into a soul which does not possess it, as if they could put sight into blind eyes. On the contrary, our own account signifies that the soul of every man does possess the power of learning the truth and the organ to see it with; and that, just as one might have to turn the whole body round in order that the eye should see light instead of darkness, so the entire soul must be turned away from the changing world, until its eye can bear to contemplate reality and that supreme splendour which we have called the Good. Hence there may well be an art whose aim would be to effect this very thing, the conversion of the soul, in the readiest way; not to put the power of sight into the soul's eye, which already has it, but to ensure that, instead of looking in the wrong direction, it is turned the way it ought to be.

Yes, it may well be so.

It looks, then, as though wisdom were different from those ordinary virtues, as they are called, which are not far removed from bodily qualities, in that they can be produced by habituation and exercise in a soul which has not possessed them from the first. Wisdom, it seems, is certainly the virtue of some diviner faculty, which never loses its power, though its use for good or harm depends on the direction towards which it is turned. You must have noticed in dishonest men with a reputation for sagacity the shrewd glance of a narrow intelligence piercing the objects to which it is directed. There is nothing wrong with their power of vision, but it has been forced into the service of evil, so that the keener its sight, the more harm it works.

Quite true.

In accordance with the fundamental theory outlined in this passage, the programme which Plato goes on to prescribe is intended gradually to habituate the eye of the soul to an ever brighter light. His primary education had been designed, without ever invoking the Ideas, which are the objects of knowledge, to inculcate by habituation a relatively but of necessity not completely stable right belief. At this stage in the *Republic* that right belief becomes in turn the starting-point for his higher education, which is to lead up thence to real knowledge, in the form of contemplation of the Ideas. As the Divided Line has taught us, the Ideas, like concrete things, can be viewed in either of two ways: either indirectly through their reflections, or in other words as an unco-ordinated plurality which is simply taken for granted and of which no account is given or attempted; or else directly, as co-ordinated and given an account of by the realization of their dependence on the Idea of the Good. And from the Cave we have learnt not only that the prisoner escaping into the outside world looks first at shadows and reflections but that he looks last of all at the sun, which stands for the Idea of the Good. We should naturally expect, therefore, that Plato's syllabus of higher education will comprise two separate stages, in the first of which the pupil will merely hypothesize the Ideas, while in the second he will set about giving an account of them. And so it proves. After their two years of military service, which follow on the end of

A ⌐ their primary education at the age of about eighteen, the
Guardians' course of higher education consists first of
E ├ ten years on the so-called 'propaedeutic' studies and then
C ├ of five years devoted solely to dialectic. Plato's Guardians
D ├ have already reached the age of thirty-five by the time
B └ their education is completed.

The propaedeutic studies consist of the five kindred
subjects of arithmetic, geometry, stereometry, astronomy
and harmonics. Irrespective of their practical uses, the
chief merit of each of these five is, to Plato's way of
thinking, that they draw the mind away from the material
and mutable objects of opinion towards immaterial and
constant realities. So much is perhaps acceptable even to
us in the first three cases: when an arithmetician says
'$2 + 2 = 4$', he is not discussing pairs of eggs or fingers, and
when a student of geometry or stereometry speaks of
circles or cubes he is not thinking of pennies or bricks.
Plato has already made that quite clear in the segment *CE*
of the Divided Line. But in the cases of harmonics and
especially astronomy the same point is at first sight far
from obvious. Astronomy may well seem to us an essentially material science, the study of the heavenly bodies.
But not so to Plato, as the following passage will show.
It begins at 529c4 and is again quoted in Cornford's version:

But how did you mean the study of astronomy to be reformed, so as to serve our purposes?
In this way. These intricate traceries in the sky are, no doubt,
the loveliest and most perfect of material things, but still part
of the visible world, and therefore they fall far short of the

true realities—the real relative velocities, in the world of pure number and all perfect geometrical figures, of the movements which carry round the bodies involved in them. These, you will agree, can be conceived by reason and thought, not seen by the eye.

Exactly.

Accordingly, we must use the embroidered heaven as a model to illustrate our study of those realities, just as one might use diagrams exquisitely drawn by some consummate artist like Daedalus. An expert in geometry, meeting with such designs, would admire their finished workmanship, but he would think it absurd to study them in all earnest with the expectation of finding in their proportions the exact ratio of any one number to another.

Of course it would be absurd.

The genuine astronomer, then, will look at the motions of the stars with the same feelings. He will admit that the sky with all that it contains has been framed by its artificer with the highest perfection of which such works are capable. But when it comes to the proportions of day to night, of day and night to month, of month to year, and of the periods of other stars to Sun and Moon and to one another, he will think it absurd to believe that these visible material things go on for ever without change or the slightest deviation, and to spend all his pains on trying to find exact truth in them.

Now you say so, I agree.

If we mean, then, to turn the soul's native intelligence to its proper use by a genuine study of astronomy, we shall proceed, as we do in geometry, by means of problems, and leave the starry heavens alone.

This remarkable passage is one of several which have been used, not without some justification, to reproach Plato as anti-scientific. His conviction of the unknowableness of material things means that his interest in astronomy

A
E
C
D
B

is not concerned to advance it as an empirical science but rather to derive from it the mathematically exact laws of perfect motion. Nevertheless his conception of astronomy, even if in a sense anti-scientific, must surely have contributed to all those physical discoveries which, although ultimately based on observation because observation revealed that there was a problem to be solved, were actually effected by abstract mathematics. But be that as it may, Plato undoubtedly thinks that astronomy leads the mind away from the material towards the immaterial. And the same is true also of harmonics, which, in Plato's opinion, is, or should be, not the study of 'audible consonances', but rather the study of 'which numbers are inherently consonant, which are not, and for what reasons' (531c1–4, tr. Cornford). Both astronomy and harmonics are, for Plato, branches of pure mathematics.

To these five subjects, then, Plato devotes ten whole years of his Guardians' education. Despite the preliminary nature implied in the name which he gives them, the name 'propaedeutic', he must have regarded them as vitally important. They seem to have been intended to serve two distinct purposes. First, they teach men how to think. They present ordinary things, such as a circular table top, to the senses and induce the mind of the beholder first to abstract the essential, the circle, from its material embodiment; then to concentrate on the universal and eternal as opposed to the particular and temporal element; and finally to set about deducing the consequences of the universals so apprehended. In the ebullient confidence inspired by his recent perception of the nature of arithmetical or geometrical truth, Plato leaps ahead in imagination and envisages everything in the universe as rigorously intelligible. He now knows by experience, and explicitly states at 526b5–9, that mathematics, by inducing abstraction, quickens and trains the mind for other subjects of study; and he includes among the sciences which demand mathematical precision both astronomy and harmonics. He therefore visualizes the five propaedeutic studies as the perfect preliminary by which men may be trained to achieve a complete, systematic and mathematically rigid understanding of the whole universe. This is his counterpart of the superficial culture dispensed in the school of Isocrates.

But as well as providing the ideal exercise in straight thinking, these five studies have also, for Plato, great significance of content. At the same time as training the faculty which is ultimately to apprehend the Ideas, they can serve also as a real introduction to the truth. When, at the end of the section devoted to the propaedeutic studies, Plato passes finally to dialectic, or when, in terms of the Divided Line, he passes from the segment *CE* to the segment *EA*, he writes as follows (531c9, tr. Cornford):

Further, I continued, this whole course of study will, I believe, contribute to the end we desire and not be labour wasted, only if it is carried to the point at which reflection can take a comprehensive view of the mutual relations and affinities which bind all these sciences together.

The five propaedeutic studies, in other words, are not arbitrarily selected and isolated each from the rest. On the contrary, each expresses a separable facet of reality and, if pursued far enough, will make its own individual contribution to an understanding of the whole truth. The only inadequacy of the kind of knowledge acquired through the propaedeutic studies is that it is necessarily hypothetical; it rests on assumptions which it takes for granted and of which it makes no attempt to give any account. In his demand that these five sciences be ultimately aimed at an understanding of their interrelationships Plato is urging, again possibly in opposition to Isocrates, that if only they be regarded not as ends in themselves but as means to a higher end, they have an invaluable purpose to serve.

The excerpt just quoted is that in which Plato at last embarks on the topic which, for the moment at least, is nearest to his heart, his science of dialectic. Characteristically he devotes to it at this stage a mere three and a half pages (531 c 9–535 a 2). Yet he acknowledges its supreme importance at the very end of that section by writing, again in Cornford's rendering:

May we conclude, then, that our account of the subjects of study is now complete? Dialectic will stand as the coping-stone of the whole structure; there is no other study that deserves to be put above it.

And in the middle of the section he has once again told us, almost in so many words, that nothing will induce him at this stage to commit his profoundest thoughts to paper. At 532 d 8 Glaucon is made to say, this time in my own translation:

Do tell us, then, what is the nature of this power which dialectic possesses, into what classes the science is divisible and what are its methods. For these would apparently lead us to the point where, when we reached it, we should rest from travel at our journey's end.

To which Socrates replies:

My dear Glaucon, you won't be able to follow any further, though not for lack of enthusiasm on my part. You would no longer be looking at an image of our theme but at the very truth—at least as it appears to me.

And Plato as usual abides by his resolution: if we wish to learn much more about his conception of dialectic, we must wait in patience for a long time yet. Perhaps no more than two of its characteristics can be inferred from any of the dialogues so far considered.

First and foremost, the word 'dialectic' was originally derived from, and remained very closely associated with, the Greek word for 'to converse'. However far Plato developed his beloved science in his later life, he seems never to have forgotten that its very basis was conversation by question and answer. That is certainly the impression that emerges from a further passage of *Epistle* VII, which is perhaps worth quoting. It begins at 344b3 and, thanks to peculiarities of both vocabulary and syntax, is by no means easy to render into English. Post (*op. cit.* p. 99) translates it as follows:

Hardly after practising detailed comparisons of names and definitions and visual and other sense-perceptions, after scrutinizing them in benevolent disputation by the use of question and answer without jealousy, at last in a flash understanding of each blazes up, and the mind, as it exerts all its powers to the limit of human capacity, is flooded with light.

The conversation involved in the pursuit of the science of dialectic may possibly on occasions be the silent dialogue of a soul conversing with itself. But even so, the fact remains that Plato's theory of knowledge led him always to believe that the right way to attain it was by putting the right question in the right words at the right moment. That much at least was a part of Plato's lifelong debt to Socrates.

To Socrates also he may have owed the generally destructive method by which dialectic proceeds. It begins, as Socrates and his interlocutors had, with the formulation of a hypothesis, which is then promptly submitted to the Socratic *elenchus* and which, if thereby overthrown, is immediately replaced by another and better hypothesis; and it continues until eventually a hypothesis is found which cannot be overthrown. Then, and not till then, the next and complementary process begins of deriving that hypothesis itself from a higher hypothesis; and again the process continues, always by question and answer, until at last it leads out, above all hypotheses, to the 'non-hypothetical first principle', the Idea of the Good. Even at that stage the *elenchus* is still applied. Only when the Good has withstood all assaults and no tests remain to be applied, then at last everything which, in the process of corroborating the Good, has been deduced from it is established as an unassailable system of knowledge. Such is the ultimate objective of the whole of Plato's syllabus of education; a mathematically precise understanding of the universe and of all that therein is. And its method too, being likewise derived from mathematics, is at least in general outline more or less intelligible. But the content of the questions and answers by which it proceeds and the nature of the successive hypotheses by which it ascends are still, at the end of the *Republic*, wrapped in the deepest mystery. Such once again is the way in which Plato saw fit to unfold to his readers his still evolving philosophy.

From the strictly metaphysical point of view the last three books of the *Republic* have little to add to those which precede them. The description in Books VIII and IX of the gradual decline of the ideal community, penetrating as it may be, is of concern to the political theorist, the sociologist and the psychologist rather than to the student of Plato's metaphysics. Even Book X has comparatively little to contribute to the central theme of this essay. It does however contain two contiguous passages which, since each takes us a step further along lines which we were following earlier, call for brief summary and comment.

In the earlier, Plato for the first time explicitly concludes that 'there is an ancient feud between philosophy and poetry' and resolves, albeit reluctantly, that poetry must be banished from the ideal state. The arguments which lead him to this conclusion cover several pages but are essentially only two, the first metaphysical, the second psychological. The gist of the metaphysical attack is straightforward enough. Since every particular object or action in the sensible world is only an image of the appropriate Idea, with infinite potentialities of distortion, every representation of such a particular must be at least twice removed from reality. Any particular bed can only

be a very imperfect embodiment of the Idea of Bed, and
any painting of that particular bed, however lifelike, can
only be a copy of a copy. Poetry, like painting, is only a
reproduction of a reproduction. Nor is that the only fault
to be found with poetry; dramatic poetry in particular is
psychologically harmful in two ways. It appeals to the
emotions rather than to the reason; and it encourages us to
sympathize with a public show of grief which in real life
we should despise as effeminate.

Quite apart from the interest of this passage as a whole,
it contains, unobtrusively embedded in it, a single sentence
which, thanks to Plato's usual reticence on the topic
concerned, assumes a significance out of all proportion to
its length. It comes near the beginning of Book x
(596a6) and runs thus:

We habitually posit a single Idea for every set of particulars
to which we apply a common name.

There can be no shadow of doubt that at the time when
Plato wrote that one sentence, though not necessarily for
the rest of his life, he thought of the world of Ideas as
co-extensive with language.

The second passage, which follows immediately on the
first (608c9–611a3), supplements the thesis of the *Phaedo*
with a new 'proof' of the immortality of the soul. Everything in the sensible world, Socrates argues, has some
peculiar evil which tends to destroy it; 'for instance,
ophthalmia for the eyes, disease for the whole body,
mildew for grain, rot for timber, rust for copper and
iron' (608e6). Anything which is not destroyed by its

own peculiar evil cannot be destroyed by anything else. If, therefore, we can point to anything which its own peculiar evil does not destroy, that thing must be indestructible. The peculiar evil of the soul is vice. But vice, though it may destroy other people's bodies, does not destroy its possessor's soul. 'So,' the argument concludes at 610e10, 'since it is not destroyed by any evil, neither its own nor anything else's, it clearly must exist for ever; and if it exists for ever, it must be immortal.' Needless to say, this latest 'proof' is no more valid than its predecessors of the *Phaedo*.

The *Republic* is generally and rightly acclaimed as Plato's masterpiece. Although Book x has something of the flavour of a series of appendices, the transitions from subject to subject being here less skilfully contrived than in earlier Books, it ends on a note worthy of the whole dialogue. After a brief account of the rewards which justice brings on earth, Plato gives us, in the Myth of Er, an imaginative picture of the fate of souls, just and unjust, after death. The myth is too remotely connected with the theme of this book to be quoted here. It is, however, quite short—less than nine pages in Cornford's translation; it is self-contained; and despite certain difficulties of detail it reveals so much of Plato's basically religious approach to philosophy that it demands to be read for its own sake.

CHAPTER II

'PHAEDRUS'

When we reach the end of the *Republic* we are confronted once again with problems of chronology, but they are not important enough for my purpose to call for detailed discussion. Today, though not always in the past, the *Phaedrus* is generally agreed to be at least later in date than the *Republic*. Stylometric considerations link it with the *Parmenides* and the *Theaetetus* and place these three dialogues in the interval, which may well have been a long one, between the *Republic* and the undoubtedly late group. The question of the relative dates of the three is more disputable. For our purposes we can afford to ignore the *Theaetetus*. Although it is at present a very popular topic of discussion among philosophers, the fact that it deliberately omits the Ideas in its epistemological investigation makes it irrelevant to our central theme. Of the other two I myself conclude, on grounds of content which will emerge in due course, that the *Phaedrus* must be the earlier. Even if I am wrong, it is without question the one that comes logically rather than chronologically next in my narrative.

As with the *Republic*, so again with the *Phaedrus*, scholars have always disagreed on its main subject and its main purpose. In ancient times, according to the commentator Hermeias, some thought its central theme was Love, some Rhetoric, some the Good and some Beauty.

Each view still seems to have its adherents. Hackforth, however, was probably not far wrong when he wrote in the Introduction to his translation and commentary (*Plato's Phaedrus*, p. 9.):

I think it is helpful to ask for the purpose rather than the subject, and I believe that there are three purposes, all important but one more important than the others. They are:

(1) To vindicate the pursuit of philosophy, in the meaning given to the word by Socrates and Plato, as the true culture of the soul . . . by contrast with the false claims of contemporary rhetoric to provide that culture. This I regard as the most important purpose.

(2) To make proposals for a reformed rhetoric, which should subserve the ends of philosophy and adopt its method.

(3) To announce a special method of philosophy—the 'dialectic' method of Collection and Division—and to exemplify this both positively (in the two speeches of Socrates) and negatively (in the speech of Lysias).

The first of these purposes, which Hackforth regards as the most important, is highly relevant; it reverts to the topic of chapter 6. Plato has by now given us, in the *Republic*, a full account of his ideal syllabus of education. In the *Phaedrus* he proceeds, in a sense, to contrast it with that of his rival, Isocrates. Possibly he even hoped, as the second purpose attributed to him by Hackforth suggests, that Isocrates might yet be induced to use his rhetorical gifts in the service of true philosophy. But however that may be, it is the third purpose which is of immediate concern to us. One quite short passage of the *Phaedrus* carries Plato's account of dialectic a step, and a very important step, further forward.

The passage in question begins at 265 c 8. The speeches on the madness of the lover's passion are over and Socrates and Phaedrus are quietly discussing the principles of style. Socrates suddenly remarks that, though in other respects his last speech had been a sportive effusion, it did 'refer in passing to a certain pair of procedures' the significance of which would repay careful study. Since the earlier reference to them had been very far from clear, Phaedrus naturally asks what these two procedures are. Socrates thereupon describes them, all too briefly, as follows:

The first consists in bringing together, in a comprehensive survey,[1] the widely scattered instances under a single Idea, so that, by a definition of each, we can clarify whatever subject we choose on any occasion for study.

And his next speech, in answer to Phaedrus' further question, what the second procedure is, opens:

The ability to divide again into classes according to natural articulations, without trying, like a bad butcher, to break up any limb.

Such is Plato's first description of the twin methods which underlay the whole of his later dialectic. It is also the prototype of every kind of classification ever since attempted.

Since dialectic, as we learnt from the Divided Line, has no truck with particulars but is concerned exclusively with the Ideas, 'the widely scattered instances' brought together by the first of the two methods must be the specific Ideas which have to be grouped under a single generic Idea—as Man, House, Pig, for instance, would be grouped

[1] συνορῶντα: cf. the epithet συνοπτικός, which is applied to the dialectician at *Republic* VII, 537 c 7.

under Animal. The procedure begins, in fact, from what I called in the last chapter the unco-ordinated plurality of Ideas at the point E of the Divided Line, and it sets about the business of co-ordinating that plurality. Its function evidently is twofold: first, as its name of 'Collection' suggests, to group together those specific Ideas which appear to belong to the same genus, and then, presumably, to divine the appropriate genus under which to classify those specific Ideas. And as soon as it has done that, the second and complementary procedure of 'Division' comes into operation. If it finds that the whole group of specific Ideas can be naturally classified under the selected genus, then that genus is established; Collection resumes at a higher level, grouping genera under higher genera; and so on, presumably, until the last Collection of all leads up to the *summum genus* itself, the Idea of the Good.

Even this brief and bald outline of the new method involves a measure both of anticipation and of conjecture. We learn a little more of the procedure from the later dialogues, notably the *Sophist*, the *Statesman* and the *Philebus*; but we never learn nearly as much as we should wish. One thing, however, is already quite clear: Plato in the *Phaedrus* is greatly impressed with the potentialities of this latest development of his metaphysical doctrine. Disproportionately short though this crucial section of the dialogue may be, it closes, only some ten lines after the end of the last excerpt, with the following eloquent speech by Socrates (266b3):

I am myself, Phaedrus, in love with these divisions and collections, in order that I may be capable of talking and thinking;

and if I reckon anybody else able to discern the one and the many as they are in nature, I follow after him 'as in the steps of a god'. And moreover, those who have this ability I have hitherto called, God knows whether rightly or wrongly, by the name of dialecticians.

Socrates is seldom made to speak with greater conviction than that.

There was one very important question which my account of the new method deliberately begged. I assumed that the ultimate aim of dialectic was still in the *Phaedrus*, as it had been in the *Republic*, the apprehension of the Idea of the Good. This assumption has often, and possibly justifiably, been questioned. Hackforth's comments on the subject, for instance, are worth quoting at some length (*op. cit.* pp. 135–6):

In *Rep.* VI and VII the goal of the dialectician's upward path is the cognition of the Form of the Good conceived as the source of all being and all knowledge, an ἀνυπόθετος ἀρχή [non-hypothetical first principle] in which supreme reality and supreme value coincide. This is not the place to attempt to amplify what Plato tells us about the ἰδέα τἀγαθοῦ [Idea of the Good]; what is relevant is to point out that Plato, for whatever reason, never afterwards speaks of it, at all events *eo nomine*; and that being so, we should not expect the dialectical method, when we meet it again, to be identical with that of the *Republic*. The μέθοδος [method] of the *Phaedrus* and later dialogues, though broad in scope and lofty enough in aim, is directed to something less tremendous (if the word may be permitted) than the μέθοδος of the *Republic*. There is not now any notion of deriving all the truths of philosophy and science from a single first principle; and we may not unreasonably conjecture that the ontological and epistemological flights of the *Republic* have been superseded by something less magnificent, but perhaps more practicable, even as were its political and social aspirations. What is now contemplated is a piecemeal approach to knowledge, consisting in a mapping out of one field after another by a classification *per genera et species* which will have the effect of at once discriminating and relating these concepts or class-names which express not mere subjective generalisations but the actual structure of reality.

The greater part of what Hackforth says in that paragraph is unquestionably true, and not least that the Idea of the Good of the *Republic* reappears thereafter, at least under that name, neither in this passage of the *Phaedrus* nor in any other later dialogue. But the apparent inference from that fact that Plato had by now lost for ever the totality of vision displayed in the *Republic* seems to me much more difficult to justify. I suspect that Hackforth himself was not completely convinced on the question, since he wrote in a footnote to the paragraph just quoted:

Of course Plato must always have postulated a Form of goodness, taken in a purely ethical sense: the moral Ideas were never abandoned, if indeed any Ideas at all were (see *Epistle* VII, 342 A ff.); moreover we know that he gave a lecture which nobody could understand, περὶ τοῦ ἀγαθοῦ [On the Good], presumably at a later date than that of the *Republic*; . . .

This is a considerable concession. If, as is generally believed and for the best of reasons, the celebrated Lecture on the Good was given late in Plato's life, no further argument is required to show that Plato continued to accord to the Good a very special position in his philosophy; while as for any suggestion that after the *Republic* Plato's vision began promptly to narrow and fade, that seems to be refuted by certain other passages of the *Phaedrus*. The section of the dialogue which contains them actually comes before the excerpt already discussed; but since it not only helps to resolve the main question arising from that excerpt but also introduces another new doctrine which Plato was to develop in later dialogues, I have chosen to defer it.

Whatever the central subject of the *Phaedrus* may be, its various theses are developed out of the three set speeches on the lover's passion. Of these three the first may possibly be, as it purports to be, a genuine work of Lysias; it is more probably a Platonic parody. The second and third, which Socrates, who recites them, is made to attribute to Phaedrus and to Stesichorus respectively, are certainly Plato's own work. The third, that in which there was the passing reference to the twin methods of Collection and Division, is much the longest—it runs to about fourteen pages—and much the most important. Its introductory section aims to show that madness is by no means always an evil. There are three distinct types of heaven-sent madness which confer on mankind the greatest of blessings: the prophetic frenzy of 'the prophetess at Delphi and the priestesses at Dodona'; the frenzy which brings healing or deliverance by revealing purificatory rites; and the frenzy which comes from the Muses and seizes, especially, the lyric poets. What we have to prove, the section concludes, is that the frenzy of the lover is also heaven-sent and also confers the greatest of blessings. 'So we must grasp the truth of the matter by seeing the nature of soul, both divine and human, and both its passive and its active properties; and the beginning of our demonstration is as follows.'

Immediately after this last sentence comes a new proof of the immortality of the soul which, since it is quite brief but very important, deserves quotation in full. It begins at 245 c 5 and is translated by Hackforth thus:

All soul is immortal; for that which is ever in motion is immortal. But that which while imparting motion is itself moved by something else can cease to be in motion, and therefore can cease to live; it is only that which moves itself that never intermits its motion, inasmuch as it cannot abandon its own nature; moreover this self-mover is the source and first principle of motion for all other things that are moved. Now a first principle cannot come into being: for while anything that comes to be must come to be from a first principle, the latter itself cannot come to be from anything whatsoever: if it did, it would cease any longer to be a first principle. Furthermore, since it does not come into being, it must be imperishable: for assuredly if a first principle were to be destroyed, nothing could come to be out of it, nor could anything bring the principle itself back into existence, seeing that a first principle is needed for anything to come into being.

The self-mover, then, is the first principle of motion: and it is as impossible that it should be destroyed as that it should come into being: were it otherwise, the whole universe, the whole of that which comes to be, would collapse into immobility, and never find another source of motion to bring it back into being.

And now that we have seen that that which is moved by itself is immortal, we shall feel no scruple in affirming that precisely that is the essence and definition of soul, to wit self-motion. Any body that has an external source of motion is soulless; but a body deriving its motion from a source within itself is animate or *besouled*, which implies that the nature of soul is what has been said.

And if this last assertion is correct, namely that 'that which moves itself' is precisely identifiable with soul, it must follow that soul is not born and does not die.

This is a pregnant passage. The doctrine, which we here encounter for the first time, of the soul's capacity for self-movement is one which Plato retained till the end of his life: it reappears, with rather startling amplifications, in the tenth book of Plato's latest dialogue, the *Laws*.[1] And although Aristotle firmly rejected the doctrine of a self-moving entity as the origin of movement and of life, and insisted that the Prime Mover must itself be wholly and eternally unmoved, this particular passage of the *Phaedrus* may well have influenced him more than he knew. At any rate not only the subject-matter, but also its logical presentation, gives us a foretaste, which we have hardly had before in Plato's writings, of the Aristotelian type of closely reasoned and concisely stated argumentation. Plato is here, without any doubt, beginning to replace the vivid vision which characterizes the middle group of dialogues with the specialized investigations of 'the more arid, undramatic, dogmatic, elaborately metaphysical, dialectical dialogues', as Shorey describes them.

The vision has not yet, however, entirely faded. The highly dialectical passage just quoted, in which Plato thinks to have proved that 'all soul is immortal', is at

[1] If, as is doubtful, the *Epinomis* is genuine, it may fairly be regarded as an appendix to the *Laws*.

196

once followed by another of Plato's imaginative myths. Plato himself at the outset describes the purpose of the myth thus (246a3, tr. Hackforth):

As to soul's immortality then we have said enough, but as to its nature there is this that must be said: what manner of thing it is would be a long tale to tell, and most assuredly a god alone could tell it; but what it resembles, that a man might tell in briefer compass: let this therefore be our manner of discourse. Let it be likened to the union of powers in a team of winged steeds and their winged charioteer.

The myth that follows reverts to the tripartite division of the soul which was first explicitly formulated, even if earlier foreshadowed in Diotima's speech in the *Symposium*, in Book IV of the *Republic*. The soul was there said to be made up of three separable constituents. Lowest came the appetitive or desirous element; next the spirited or passionate; and highest the rational or intellectual. And the various virtues, according to the *Republic*, consisted in the correct harmony between these three parts of the soul. Such is the basis of the *Phaedrus* myth. The charioteer, of course, represents the reason, striving to control the ill-paired steeds.

Now all the gods' steeds and all their charioteers are good, and of good stock; but with other beings it is not wholly so. With us men . . . one of them is noble and good, and of good stock, while the other has the opposite character, and his stock is opposite. Hence the task of our charioteer is difficult and troublesome.

In the procession of souls which the myth goes on to describe, the souls of men are 'marshalled in eleven companies' according to their individual characters, and the 'ruler gods lead their several companies, each according to his rank'. And

behold they climb the steep ascent even unto the summit of the arch that supports the heavens; and easy is that ascent for the chariots of the gods, for that they are well-balanced and readily guided; but for the others it is hard, by reason of the heaviness of the steed of wickedness, which pulls down his driver with his weight, except that driver have schooled him well.

And now there awaits the soul the extreme of her toil and struggling. For the souls that are called immortal, so soon as they are at the summit, come forth and stand upon the back of the world: and straightway the revolving heaven carries them round, and they look upon the regions without. . . . It is there that true Being dwells, without colour or shape, that cannot be touched; reason alone, the soul's pilot, can behold it, and all true knowledge is knowledge thereof. . . .

Now . . . the mind of a god is nourished by reason and knowledge. . . . While she is borne round she discerns justice, its very self, and likewise temperance, and knowledge, not the knowledge that is neighbour to Becoming and varies with the various objects to which we commonly ascribe being, but the veritable knowledge of Being that veritably is. . . . Such is the life of the gods: of the other souls that which best follows a god and becomes most like thereunto raises her charioteer's head into the outer region and is carried round with the gods in the revolution, but being confounded by her steeds she has much ado to discern the things that are; another now rises, and now sinks, and by reason of her unruly steeds sees in part, but in part sees not. As for the rest, though all are eager to reach the heights and seek to follow, they are not able: sucked down as they travel they trample and tread upon one another, this one striving to outstrip that. Thus confusion ensues, and conflict and grievous sweat: whereupon, with their charioteers powerless, many are lamed, and many have their wings all broken; and for all their toiling they are baulked, every one, of the full vision of Being, and departing therefrom, they feed upon the food of semblance.

I have abridged this particular myth to eliminate certain complications that are irrelevant to my theme. Like the speech of Diotima in the *Symposium*, the myth of the *Phaedrus* can be allowed to speak largely for itself. Here, clearly, we have Plato's poetical or imaginative account of how the soul of man first came to know those realities the recollection of which, according to the doctrine of the *Meno*, constitutes knowledge as opposed to right belief. However much Plato's philosophy may have been broadened and strengthened in the dialogues of the middle group, its basis is still the same in the *Phaedrus* as it had been when, in the *Meno*, he first began to expound his own positive views. The soul is immortal; the reason is akin to the gods; every soul before incarnation has enjoyed at least a partial glimpse of reality; all learning is a recollection of that glimpse.

And for the matter of that, in spite of the tenth Book of the *Republic*, the poet in Plato, the visionary mystic, is still in the *Phaedrus* vigorously alive. The same can hardly be said of the *Parmenides*, which we must consider in the next chapter. If I am right in believing that the *Phaedrus* is earlier than the *Parmenides*, and if for the moment we ignore the *Timaeus*, then the *Phaedrus* gives us the last bright flash of Plato's vision while the introductory section of the *Parmenides* inaugurates the stage of his life in which he was diligently seeking for a logical and metaphysical defence for what he had earlier seen.

PART III

CHAPTER 12

'PARMENIDES'

For the twenty years following his first visit to Sicily in
388–7 B.C. Plato had lived, as head of the Academy, a busy
but cloistered life. However much he may have written
during those twenty years—a question on which unanimity
is unlikely to be ever attained—he must before the end of
them have come to feel that he had found a mission which
would keep him happily occupied until the end of his days.
Such a hope, however, suddenly proved false. In 367
Dionysius I, tyrant of Syracuse, perhaps assisted by his
self-seeking doctors, died an apparently natural death. He
was succeeded by his son of the same name, who was then,
probably, in his late twenties and who seems to have
been neither particularly clever nor trained for his future
responsibilities. According to Plutarch, who, next to
Epistle VII, is our best source of information on this period
of Sicilian history, the elder Dionysius had deliberately
denied his son the advantages of any sort of education.

Fearing that if he should get wisdom and associate with men
of sense, he would plot against him and rob him of his power,
he used to keep him closely shut up at home, where, through
lack of association with others and in ignorance of affairs, as
we are told, he made little waggons and lampstands and
wooden chairs and tables [*Dion* IX, tr. Perrin].

Although, as Plutarch's own language suggests, this sentence is not to be relied on as historical evidence, it shows

that Dionysius II was generally regarded from the outset as ill equipped for his exacting duties. No wonder that Plato hesitated before he was again drawn, against all his instincts, into the political arena.

Epistle VII continues, from the point to which we followed it in Part I, with an account, somewhat incoherent and interrupted by a sequence of philosophical digressions, of Plato's second and third visits to Syracuse. Dion, who was not only the young tyrant's uncle but also the most influential member of his government, saw at last a godsent opportunity to convert a despot to philosophy. He wrote to Plato, according to *Epistle* VII, saying: 'What better occasion can we expect than that which, by divine chance, has now come our way? . . . At this moment, if ever, our whole hope will be achieved: the same men will be at once philosophers and rulers of great cities' (327e–328b). With many misgivings, and with little hope of turning Dionysius II into a philosopher-king, Plato eventually acceded to Dion's request and left Athens for Syracuse. He could not, at this crucial juncture, desert the principles which he had for ever been preaching and he had no option, in the interests of the Academy, but to demonstrate to his critics that he practised what he preached.

The next part of the melancholy narrative of *Epistle* VII runs as follows:

When I arrived—for I must be brief—I found Dionysius' entourage seething with faction and with slanderous reports to the tyrant about Dion. I defended him to the best of my ability, but there was little I could do. Within about four months of my arrival Dionysius accused Dion of plotting against the tyranny, put him aboard a small boat and exiled him in disgrace. After that, all Dion's friends were afraid lest Dionysius should accuse and punish any one of us as an accomplice in the plot, and in my own case a rumour got around in Syracuse that I had been put to death by Dionysius because I was responsible for all these recent events [329 b–d].

Having successfully rid himself of Dion, Dionysius next took steps, for the sake of his own reputation, to prevent Plato's departure.

He took me and settled me in the citadel, whence no ship's captain would conceivably have taken me aboard unless Dionysius not only did nothing to prevent it but actually sent a messenger with express orders to take me. Otherwise no merchant or emigration officer would have allowed me to leave by myself, but would have arrested me on the spot and taken me back to Dionysius; especially since the rumour was now abroad—the very opposite of the earlier one—that Dionysius was exceptionally fond of Plato [329 e–330 a].

Eventually, however,

I persuaded Dionysius, by every means in my power, to let me go; but when peace should be made—for there was war in Sicily at the time—we both agreed to certain terms. Dionysius promised to send for Dion and me again, as soon as he had established his government more securely; and meanwhile he begged Dion not to think that he had been exiled but only temporarily rusticated. On such terms I for my part agreed to return [338 a–b].

When peace was restored in Sicily, Dionysius of course proved false to his word. He sent for Plato again, some five years after his return from the second visit, but he did not send for Dion. Plato naturally, to start with, declined the invitation: 'It seemed safer at that stage to let Dion and Dionysius go their own ways' (338c). But under a heavy bombardment from every imaginable quarter Plato again yielded. Dion as well as Dionysius had been imploring him to go; Archytas and the Tarentines, presumably from political motives, had added powerful pleas; even the Athenians were 'virtually pushing me out with their entreaties' (339d); above all, Dionysius was rumoured to have taken to philosophy and was so eager for Plato's guidance that he had sent a trireme, loaded with suitable emissaries and letters, to convey Plato in comparative comfort to his destination.

Needless to say the third visit, of which *Epistle* VII gives us a relatively full account, was no more successful than the second. On his arrival in Syracuse Plato gave Dionysius a prefabricated test which revealed at once that he had no natural aptitude for philosophy. Dion's prospects, so far from being improved by Plato's intermediacy, deteriorated steadily to the point at which he was constrained to raise a mercenary army in the Peloponnese and mount a successful invasion of Syracuse. Plato himself spent the latter part of his visit, still vainly trying to do good works, 'living outside the acropolis amongst the mercenaries', who might at any moment have vented their indiscriminate rebelliousness against him. Eventually, in real danger,

I sent a message to Archytas and my other friends at Tarentum telling them of my present position. They trumped up some excuse for an embassy from their city and sent a thirty-oared ship with Lamiscus, one of their party, aboard. When he arrived, he pleaded with Dionysius on my behalf, saying that I wanted to leave and begging him to do nothing to prevent it. Dionysius consented and despatched me with my fare. As for Dion's property [which Dionysius had arbitrarily confiscated since Plato's latest arrival in Syracuse], I gave up asking for it myself and nobody gave it back to him [350a–b].

Two such disillusioning journeys were bound to have had an effect on any man. For Plato, the most natural result would be that he started to think yet again about the practicability of converting an already established tyrant to philosophy and thereby bringing to birth, under the rule of a philosopher-king, the ideal state envisaged in the *Republic*. One conjecture at least, provided it is recognized as such, seems fairly safe. Plato may well have realized, by the time he returned to Athens after the first of the two journeys, that in this imperfect world the perfect state was an unattainable ideal. Though he still had occasional glimpses of his earlier all-embracing vision, the *Laws*, which is the last work that can be confidently attributed to him, reflects the kind of practical disillusionment which the last two visits to Syracuse must have induced. In place of the inspired vision of the *Republic*, the *Laws* gives us, for the most part, only realistic proposals for the establishment and maintenance of the second-best state. The final group of dialogues, from the *Parmenides* to the *Laws*, can be expected progressively to replace mysticism with realism. Many scholars have yielded to the obvious temptation and concluded that the striking differences, in matter and style alike, between the middle and the late groups of dialogues are attributable, in part at least, to

Plato's renewed involvement in the intrigues of the Syracusan court.

The *Parmenides* inaugurates the new phase with dramatic abruptness. The greater part of the dialogue is of an unprecedented obscurity, which is itself significant: even its main motive has been very variously interpreted and is still disputed. But its introduction, which is all that is here relevant, can once more, despite much recent and controversial discussion of its purpose, be allowed to speak largely for itself.

After a brief prefatory narrative, the dialogue begins with Zeno reading his paradoxical treatise. 'If things are many', he maintains, 'they must be both like and unlike. But that is impossible: unlike things cannot be like, nor like things unlike.' Whereupon the young Socrates is represented as offering the theory of Ideas, just as it was first formulated in the *Phaedo*, as the explanation of how one thing can have two contrary characters. He suggests that things are separable into three classes: Ideas such as Likeness and Unlikeness; things such as the mathematician's 'Equals', mentioned in the *Phaedo* at 74 c 1, which are defined as essentially like or unlike; and finally concrete things, which can participate in two contrary Ideas at the same time, as Simmias, for instance, is said, again in the *Phaedo* (102), to participate in Tallness as compared with the share of Shortness in Socrates but in Shortness as compared with the share of Tallness in Phaedo.[1]

---

[1] The two illustrations, like the whole of the translation of the *Parmenides*, are borrowed from Cornford's *Plato and Parmenides*, pp. 63–107.

Zeno, Socrates says, is confusing these three separate classes and mistakenly maintaining that, because the third class can admittedly have two opposite characteristics at the same time, the other two classes must do likewise. The theory of Ideas, he claims, solves Zeno's conundrums.

At this juncture the elderly Parmenides enters the discussion with a series of searching questions about the Ideas. The passage which follows is too long to be quoted in full, but most of it is so pertinent that it cannot be omitted. The whole section starts at 130a 3 as follows:

While Socrates was speaking, Pythodorus said he was expecting every moment that Parmenides and Zeno would be annoyed; but they listened very attentively and kept on exchanging glances and smiles in admiration of Socrates. When he ended, Parmenides expressed this feeling: Socrates, he said, your eagerness for discussion is admirable. And now tell me: have you yourself drawn this distinction you speak of and separated apart on the one side Ideas[1] themselves and on the other the things that share in them? Do you believe there is such a thing as Likeness itself apart from the likeness that we possess, and so on with Unity and Plurality and all the terms in Zeno's argument that you have just been listening to?

Certainly I do, said Socrates.

And also in cases like these, asked Parmenides: is there, for example, an Idea of Rightness or of Beauty or of Goodness, and of all such things?

Yes.

And again, an Idea of Man, apart from ourselves and all other men like us—an Idea of Man as something by itself? Or an Idea of Fire or of Water?

I have often been puzzled about those things, Parmenides,

[1] For the sake of consistency I have throughout this passage substituted 'Ideas' for Cornford's 'Forms'.

whether one should say that the same thing is true in their case or not.

Are you also puzzled, Socrates, about cases that may be thought absurd, such as hair or mud or dirt or any other trivial and undignified objects? Are you doubtful whether or not to assert that each of these has a separate Idea distinct from things like those we handle?

Not at all, said Socrates; in these cases, the things are just the things we see; it would surely be too absurd to suppose that they have an Idea. All the same, I have sometimes been troubled by a doubt whether what is true in one case may not be true in all. Then, when I have reached that point, I am driven to retreat, for fear of tumbling into a bottomless pit of nonsense. Anyhow, I get back to the things we were just now speaking of as having Ideas, and occupy my time with thinking about them.

That, replied Parmenides, is because you are still young, Socrates, and philosophy has not yet taken hold of you so firmly as I believe it will some day. You will not despise any of these objects then; but at present your youth makes you still pay attention to what the world will think.

The purport of this first section is plain enough. Parmenides asks simply what classes of Ideas are to be recognized, and Socrates' answer suggests that Plato felt that the world of Ideas was liable to be too narrowly restricted. Socrates admits without hesitation such 'Highest Classes',[1] as they are later called in the *Sophist*, as Likeness and Unlikeness or Unity and Plurality, and also the moral Ideas with which Plato has in his earlier dialogues been primarily concerned. He hesitates about Ideas of natural species and of the elements, but as Plato

---

[1] μέγιστα γένη.

admits both classes in later dialogues we can safely conclude that Socrates' hesitation is only a dramatic device.
And since Parmenides dismisses as unphilosophical Socrates' objection to the final class of Ideas, those of natural
substances such as hair and dirt, we can hardly doubt that
Plato recognized them as well. Although there are obvious omissions in the present list, such as Ideas of manu-
factured articles like Shuttle or Bed, it nevertheless leaves
a strong impression that the verdict of *Republic* X is still
valid: 'We habitually posit a single Idea for every set of
particulars to which we apply a common name.' Nothing that Plato himself wrote after the *Parmenides* gain-
says that conclusion.

Next comes a searching criticism of the metaphor of
participation (130e4):

However that may be, tell me this. You say you hold that
there exist certain Ideas, of which these other things come to
partake and so to be called after their names: by coming to
partake of Likeness or Largeness or Beauty or Justice, they
become like or large or beautiful or just?

Certainly, said Socrates.

Then each thing that partakes receives as its share either the
Idea as a whole or a part of it? Or can there be any other way
of partaking besides this?

No, how could there be?

Do you hold, then, that the Idea as a whole, a single thing,
is in each of the many, or how?

Why should it not be in each, Parmenides?

If so, an Idea which is one and the same will be at the same
time, as a whole, in a number of things which are separate,
and consequently will be separate from itself.

No, it would not, replied Socrates, if it were like one and

the same day, which is in many places at the same time and nevertheless is not separate from itself. Suppose any given Idea is in them all at the same time as one and the same thing in that way.

I like the way you make out that one and the same thing is in many places at once, Socrates. You might as well spread a sail over a number of people and then say that the one sail as a whole was over them all. Don't you think that is a fair analogy?

Perhaps it is.

Then would the sail as a whole be over each man, or only a part over one, another part over another?

Only a part.

In that case, Socrates, the Ideas themselves must be divisible into parts, and the things which have a share in them will have a part for their share. Only a part of any given Idea, and no longer the whole of it, will be in each thing.

Evidently, on that showing.

Are you, then, prepared to assert that we shall find the single Idea actually being divided? Will it still be one?

Certainly not.

No, for consider this. Suppose that it is Largeness itself that you are going to divide into parts, and that each of the many large things is to be large by virtue of a part of Largeness which is smaller than Largeness itself. Will not that seem unreasonable?

It will indeed.

And again, if it is Equality that a thing receives some small part of, will that part, which is less than Equality itself, make its possessor equal to something else?

No, that is impossible.

Well, take Smallness: is one of us to have a portion of Smallness, and is Smallness to be larger than that portion, which is a part of it? On this supposition again Smallness itself will be larger, and anything to which the portion taken is added will be smaller, and not larger, than it was before.

That cannot be so.

Well then, Socrates, how are the other things going to partake of your Ideas, if they can partake of them neither in part nor as wholes?

Really, said Socrates, it seems no easy matter to determine in any way.

The purport is again clear enough. Parmenides criticizes the theory that many particulars can participate in a single indivisible Idea by arguing that either the whole Idea must be in each of the many particulars, in which case it is no longer single, or else a part of the Idea is in each, in which case it is no longer indivisible. He interprets the metaphor of participation, in other words, in a material sense, and Plato's choice of examples, Largeness, Equality and Smallness, is presumably intended to show that such an interpretation is misguided. Obscure as the nature of participation may be, we must think of it, Plato seems to mean, as an immaterial relationship which is not negated by materialistic objections.

The same materialistic interpretation underlies Parmenides' next criticism, a criticism that was to be repeated by Aristotle in his discussions of the theory of Ideas and given the name 'the argument of the Third Man'. Parmenides continues thus:

Again, there is another question.

What is that?

How do you feel about this? I imagine your ground for believing in a single Idea in each case is this: when it seems to you that a number of things are large, there seems, I suppose, to be a certain single character which is the same when you look at them all; hence you think that Largeness is a single thing.

True, he replied.

But now take Largeness itself and the other things which are large. Suppose you look at all these in the same way in your mind's eye, will not yet another unity make its appearance— a Largeness by virtue of which they all appear large?

So it would seem.

If so, a second Idea of Largeness will present itself, over and above Largeness itself and the things that share in it; and again, covering all these, yet another, which will make all of them large. So each of your Ideas will no longer be one, but an indefinite number.

Parmenides is here assuming that the Idea of Largeness, being itself the perfect instance of that Idea, is in effect yet one more of the large things which it has been postulated to explain. Aristotle accepted the assumption as valid, but can Plato himself have done so? Even if he felt that Parmenides' argument was fallacious, he nevertheless represents the young Socrates as unable to detect the fallacy. Yet not only the sequel in the *Parmenides*, but also the continued use of the theory of Ideas in later dialogues, suggests that to Plato's thinking this argument, like its predecessor and for much the same reason, must admit of a cogent answer.

At this stage in the discussion Socrates attempts to evade the difficulty by two alternative suggestions of the utmost significance. Here is the first:

But, Parmenides, said Socrates, may it not be that each of these Ideas is a thought, which cannot properly exist anywhere but in a mind? In that way each of them can be one and the statements that have just been made would no longer be true of it.

214

Then, is each Idea one of these thoughts and yet a thought of nothing?

No, that is impossible.

So it is a thought of something?

Yes.

Of something that exists or of something that does not?

Of something that exists.[1]

In fact, of some *one* thing which that thought observes to cover all the cases, as being a certain single character?

Yes.

Then will not this thing that is thought of as being one and always the same in all cases be an Idea?

That again seems to follow.

So Plato rapidly disposes of a possible misinterpretation— one which, incidentally, often arises from the use of the term 'Idea' in preference to 'Form'. Platonic Ideas are not mere thoughts in a mind, not even in God's mind; they have a substantial existence of their own.

After a further relatively unimportant objection from Parmenides to his first suggestion, Socrates goes on at once to his second:

But, Parmenides, the best I can make of the matter is this: that these Ideas are as it were patterns fixed in the nature of things; the other things are made in their image and are likenesses; and this participation they come to have in the Ideas is nothing but their being made in their image.

Well, if a thing is made in the image of the Idea, can that Idea fail to be like the image of it, in so far as the image was made in its likeness? If a thing is like, must it not be like something that is like it?

[1] In these two sentences I have substituted 'exists' for Cornford's 'is'.

It must.

And must not the thing which is like share with the thing that is like it in one and the same character?

Yes.

And will not that in which the like things share, so as to be alike, be just the Idea itself that you spoke of?

Certainly.

If so, nothing can be like the Idea, nor can the Idea be like anything. Otherwise a second Idea will always make its appearance over and above the first Idea; and if that second Idea is like anything, yet a third; and there will be no end to this emergence of fresh Ideas, if the Idea is to be like the thing that partakes of it.

Quite true.

It follows that the other things do not partake of Ideas by being like them; we must look for some other means by which they partake.

So it seems.

Once more Socrates is represented as baffled; yet, according to some commentators, Parmenides' fallacy is blatant. As Cornford writes (*op. cit.* pp. 93-4): 'Proclus pointed out that the relation of copy to original is not *merely* one of likeness; the copy is derived from the original. The reflection of my face in a glass is a copy of my face and like my face; my face is like the reflection, but not a copy of it.' And he adds that Plato himself must have been aware of the fallacy, since 'he did not give up speaking of Forms as patterns in the nature of things'. Yet in that case once again, why did Aristotle continue to regard Parmenides' objection as valid?

The final objection that Parmenides raises is too long and complicated to be quoted in full. He professes to

prove that the Ideas, even if they exist, can have no relation whatever to the particulars of our world and cannot
possibly be knowable to men. But before he embarks on
this last argument he makes the following significant
remark (133 b 4):

Suppose someone should say that the Ideas, if they are such as
we are saying they must be, cannot even be known. One
could not convince him that he was mistaken in that objection,
unless he chanced to be a man of wide experience and natural
ability, and were willing to follow one through a long and
remote train of argument.

We could hardly ask for a broader hint: only his youth
and inexperience reduce Socrates to submission.

That brings us to the end of Parmenides' searching
critique, much of which may have been inspired by discussions in the Academy. The most important conclusions
that apparently emerge from it are these: first, that the
study of the world of Ideas was in danger of being unduly
restricted; second, that the relationship described as
participation needed further thought, and especially the
hypothesis that it consisted in the imitation of a model by
its copies; third, that the Ideas cannot be dismissed as mere
thoughts but must have a substantial existence; and finally
that, whatever objective validity any of Parmenides' criticisms may possess, Plato himself, who either invented
them or borrowed them from his critics, somehow
managed to remain undismayed. This last point may be
thought to need further substantiation, which is promptly
forthcoming in the sequel. For Parmenides, though he
has now concluded his criticism, has more to add of the

utmost significance. The passage continues as follows (134e9):

And yet, Socrates, Parmenides went on, these difficulties and many more besides are inevitably involved in the Ideas, if these characters of things really exist and one is going to distinguish each Idea as a thing just by itself. The result is that the hearer is perplexed and inclined either to question their existence, or to contend that, if they do exist, they must certainly be unknowable by our human nature. Moreover, there seems to be some weight in these objections, and, as we were saying, it is extraordinarily difficult to convert the objector. Only a man of exceptional gifts will be able to see that an Idea, or essence just by itself, does exist in each case; and it will require someone still more remarkable to discover it and to instruct another who has thoroughly examined all these difficulties.

I admit that, Parmenides; I quite agree with what you are saying.

But on the other hand, Parmenides continued, if, in view of all these difficulties and others like them, a man refuses to admit that Ideas of things exist or to distinguish a definite Idea in every case, he will have nothing on which to fix his thought, so long as he will not allow that each thing has a character which is always the same; and in so doing he will completely destroy the significance of all discourse. But of that consequence I think you are only too well aware.

True.

What are you going to do about philosophy, then? Where will you turn while the answers to these questions remain unknown?

I can see no way out at the present moment.

That is because you are undertaking to define 'Beautiful', 'Just', 'Good', and other particular Ideas, too soon, before you have had a preliminary training. I noticed that the other day when I heard you talking here with Aristoteles. Believe me, there is something noble and inspired in your passion for argument; but you must make an effort to submit yourself, while you are still young, to a severer training in what the world calls idle talk and condemns as useless. Otherwise the truth will escape you.

That passage, especially when coupled with one from the *Sophist* to be discussed later, should dispose of any suggestion that in the *Parmenides* Plato is renouncing the theory of Ideas. On the contrary, what he is doing in this introductory section of the dialogue is to urge that the theory as it was first expounded in the *Phaedo* calls for a great deal of further specialized investigation. The theory of the *Phaedo* is still of immense importance, because it first postulated the separate existence of, for example, Beauty itself and explained the beauty of beautiful things by reference to that ideal Beauty. But how much it left unexplained! It gave no inkling how or why beautiful things should ever have begun to partake in Beauty itself. It simply set up two separate worlds, the world of Ideas and the sensible world, and dogmatically asserted, without any explanation, a mysterious relation between the two. Nor did it offer any account whatever of the relationship between one Idea and another. Since the incomplete theory of the *Phaedo*, rather than the more detailed and elaborate theory of the *Republic*, is the object of Parmenides' attack, we ought not to be surprised to find Plato here saying, as in effect he makes Parmenides say: 'True, the Ideas must exist, or else all thought and language are meaningless; but you will not be able to defend their existence against an objector until you have undergone a preliminary training.' The vital question at this stage is, What is the nature of this preliminary training?

Cornford gives us the answer, or as much of an answer as is yet justified, in the following two sentences (*op. cit.* pp. 103–4). First: 'The suggestion is that, before setting out to define some particular Form, there is need to study the general assumptions involved in the assertion that such a Form exists and can be defined.' And second, a little later: 'Since every definition is a statement about a Form entirely in terms of other Forms, we may suspect that the preliminary exercise needed before any definition is undertaken will have some bearing on that question of the relation of Forms among themselves.' That, in brief, is all that we can so far safely surmise. But fortunately Parmenides has still not concluded his advice.

The passage continues as follows (135 d 7):

What form, then, should this exercise take, Parmenides?

The Form that Zeno used in the treatise you have been listening to. With this exception: there was one thing you said to him which impressed me very much: you would not allow the survey to be confined to visible things or to range only over that field; it was to extend to those objects which are specially apprehended by discourse and can be regarded as Ideas.

Yes, because in that other field there seems to be no difficulty about showing that things are both like and unlike and have any other character you please.

You are right. But there is one thing more you must do. If you want to be thoroughly exercised, you must not merely make the supposition that such and such a thing *is* and then consider the consequences; you must also take the supposition that that same thing *is not*.

How do you mean?

Take, if you like, the supposition that Zeno made: '*If there is a plurality of things.*' You must consider what consequences must follow both for those many things with reference to one another and to the One, and also for the One with reference to itself and to the many. Then again, on the supposition that *there is not a plurality*, you must consider what will follow both for the One and for the many, with reference to themselves and to each other. Or, once more, if you suppose that 'Likeness exists', or 'does not exist', what will follow on either supposition both for the terms supposed and for other things, with reference to themselves and to each other. And so again with Unlikeness, Motion and Rest, Coming-to-be and Perishing, and Being and Not-being themselves. In a word, whenever you suppose that anything whatsoever exists or does not exist or has any other character, you ought to consider the consequences with reference to itself and to any one of the other things that you may select, or several of them, or all of them together; and again you must study these others with reference both to one another and to any one thing you may select, whether you have assumed the thing to exist or not to exist, if you are really going to make out the truth after a complete course of discipline.

There would be no end to such an undertaking, Parmenides; and I don't altogether understand.

The preliminary training required before we can defend the theory of Ideas against an objector is evidently to consist of two stages. We have first to adopt Zeno's method of taking a hypothesis, such as that plurality exists, and deducing all its consequences, and we have to extend it to cover the ideal as well as the sensible world. And then we have to take also the contrary hypothesis, that plurality does not exist, and deduce its consequences also. This second stage, of course, completely transforms the method as it had been employed by Zeno. For whereas Zeno's aim had always been destructive, the *reductio ad absurdum* of his pluralist opponents' hypotheses, the revised method has become, potentially at least, positive and constructive. It now ought, even if it does not seem to do so in the remainder of the *Parmenides*, to result in the establishment of one or the other of the contrary hypotheses as true.

So much for the method itself; but what of its content? All that we can learn on that subject from the whole of the *Parmenides* is contained in the sentences just quoted, in which we are given as examples of the kind of hypothesis to be examined the following five pairs of opposite concepts: Unity and Plurality, Likeness and Unlikeness, Rest and Motion, Being and Not-being, Coming-to-be and Perishing. These five pairs had, as a matter of fact, been of particular concern to the historic Parmenides. Of the first four pairs he had in his *Way of Truth*, which started from the solitary premise 'It is', established the existence of the former member and rejected the latter; the fifth pair had been alike rejected in the single line (Fr. 8, 21):

So is coming-to-be extinguished and perishing unimaginable.

They were to be of equal concern to Plato in his later life.

This whole introductory section of the *Parmenides*, if only it is read and studied in close connection with the latter half of the *Phaedo*, is, I believe, less paradoxical than it may otherwise appear. In the *Phaedo*, when Plato first propounds his theory of Ideas, his chief contention is that only by postulating a separate and independently existing Idea for every class or characteristic of particulars can we give a rational account of those particulars. But, he suggests, this may not yet be a complete explanation of reality. If we have, in answer to an objector, to give an account of the Ideas themselves, then we must go on postulating higher and higher hypotheses until we come to 'something satisfactory'. In the *Parmenides* the theory as expounded in the *Phaedo* is subjected to a series of at least superficially damaging criticisms. Plato himself may conceivably, as Cornford suggests, have believed that the majority of these criticisms were based upon fallacies; yet he represents the young Socrates as wholly unable to defend the theory of Ideas against them. And even Aristotle, after nineteen years of the closest association with Plato, was in the end reluctantly constrained to reject the theory of Ideas not least because of the objections to it put by Plato himself into the mouth of Parmenides. We here encounter a problem to which a generally acceptable solution may never be found. Can Plato have seen, or thought that he saw, a valid answer to his own critique and yet for some inscrutable reason have failed to impart it to the ablest of his pupils? Or had he, by this stage of his life, become so enamoured of the Ideas that, despite the rational objections which he knew could be brought against them, he still clung to them by an act of faith? We cannot say. But however that may be, the *Parmenides*, like the *Republic* even if in a more provocative fashion, still seems to me to amplify rather than to repudiate the conclusions of the *Phaedo*. The Ideas, while in a sense the ultimate reality, are not just an indefinite collection of separate entities of which no more can be said than that they exist. They must be able to combine one with another and a hierarchy must be detectable in the ideal world by which the higher levels of reality embrace the lower and co-ordinate them into an intelligible order. Henceforth Plato will devote much time and thought to the investigation of the extent and nature of these higher levels.[1]

[1] I have omitted from my account the very latest developments of Plato's metaphysics, which, apart from certain tentative presentiments in the *Philebus*, must in the main be reconstructed from Aristotle's terse comments on the so-called 'Unwritten Doctrines'. Any reader who wishes to pursue this difficult subject further should turn first to chapters IX–XVII of *Plato's Theory of Ideas* by Sir David Ross.

CHAPTER 13

'SOPHIST' AND 'TIMAEUS'

The dialogues usually assigned to the last group of Plato's writings are the *Sophist* and the *Statesman*, the *Timaeus* and the unfinished *Critias*, the *Philebus*, the *Laws*. Although each of these six contains passages that throw light on the later evolution of his metaphysics, every major development is discernible in two only. A few excerpts from the *Sophist* teach us almost all that we can ever learn about the procedure of Plato's later dialectic, while the *Timaeus* as a whole, if it is indeed as late as has been generally supposed, gives us virtually his final assessment of the status and function both of the Ideas and of soul.

The first relevant passage from the *Sophist* is the one near the beginning (218d–221c) in which the stranger from Elea, who has usurped Socrates' place as protagonist, gives us an illustration of the twin methods of the *Phaedrus*, Collection and Division, by defining the Angler. He at once reveals one characteristic of the good dialectician, his synoptic view, by his choice of Art, rather than of any narrower sub-genus, as the *summum genus* from which to start the Division. Art is first divided into the art of making and the art of acquiring, the latter is again subdivided, and the process of dichotomy is continued until we arrive at the definition of angling as, in an abbreviated version, the art of acquiring by stealthy capture creatures which inhabit water, the capture being effected in daylight by a stroke from above. This particular illustration is of course flippant, but in spite of that the passage is of the greatest importance. Not only does it put upon paper the prototype of all formal classification; it also presents us with the first example, to be laboriously followed, with little apparent profit, in the remainder of the *Sophist* and throughout the *Statesman*, of what Plato intended by the methods of Collection and Division. Collection is evidently to consist in bringing together specific Ideas under a common generic Idea, Division in the hierarchical arrangement under that generic Idea of all its constituent sub-genera and species. And these are methods that can and will be applied to subjects of greater metaphysical importance than angling.

The other relevant section of the *Sophist* is the long one from the middle of the dialogue (251a–259d) in which the problem is raised, and answered, of whether or not, and if so how, Ideas can combine among themselves. The passage opens with the Stranger dismissing as trivial, as it was dismissed in the *Parmenides* and will be again in the *Philebus*, the old problem of how one individual thing can have many 'names' or characteristics. We are not here concerned, as we were in the *Phaedo*, with the relation of the particulars of the sensible world to the Ideas, but rather with the relation of the Ideas among themselves. Accordingly the first question to be answered is whether no Idea can ever combine with any other, whether every Idea can combine with every other, or, finally, whether some Ideas will combine and others not. The Stranger tackles the problem by taking as his example three of the

Ideas already encountered in the 'preliminary training' of the *Parmenides*, those of Motion, Rest and Existence. If no Ideas can combine, he argues, then neither Motion nor Rest can partake of Existence; that disposes of the first of the three possibilities. Again, if all Ideas can combine, then 'Motion itself would come to a standstill and Rest itself would be in motion' (252d6). So we quickly reach the conclusion that some Ideas are compatible, others not. 'Then,' says the Stranger, '. . . they might be said to be in the same case with the letters of the alphabet. Some of these cannot be conjoined, others will fit together' (252e9).[1] But in the case of the letters of the alphabet a special art is required, namely grammar, to determine which can combine with which; and likewise the art of music is a prerequisite before we can understand which sounds will blend and which will not. 'And we shall find differences of the same sort between competence and incompetence in any other art.' But if that is so, the Stranger goes on, some art or science must surely exist to enable us to determine which Ideas are consonant and which incompatible; the science, needless to say, of dialectic. For, in Plato's own words (253d1):

STRANGER: Dividing according to Kinds, not taking the same Idea for a different one or a different one for the same —is not that the business of the science of Dialectic?

THEAETETUS: Yes.

STR.: And the man who can do that discerns clearly *one* Idea everywhere extended throughout many, where each one lies apart, and *many* Ideas, different from one another,

[1] All the citations from Plato in this chapter are from Cornford's books *Plato's Theory of Knowledge* and *Plato's Cosmology*.

embraced from without by one Idea; and again *one* Idea
connected in a unity through many wholes, and *many* Ideas,
entirely marked off apart. That means knowing how to
distinguish, Kind by Kind, in what ways the several Kinds
can or can not combine.

TH.: Most certainly.

STR.: And the only person, I imagine, to whom you would
allow this mastery of Dialectic is the pure and rightful lover
of wisdom.

TH.: To whom else could it be allowed?[1]

Even by Plato's standards that passage is a masterpiece
of compression. Legitimately expanded, the Stranger's
middle speech alone might run to several pages.

What the first sentence of the speech presents is a more
detailed, if still an obscure, account of the procedure of
dialectic; an account from a slightly different angle from
that of the *Phaedrus* but in full accord with it. The first
half describes Collection, though this time the result
rather than the process; and what it tells us amounts
briefly (but less briefly than Plato saw fit to express it) to
this. The dialectician, after he has completed his Collection, can survey the result in either of two ways. Looking
at it from above, as it were, he can see how a single
generic Idea, such as Art in the earlier illustration, per-
vades all its distinct constituent species; and at the same
time, looking at it from below, he can see how the many
and various specific Ideas can, despite their differences, be

---

[1] I have again, for the sake of consistency, substituted 'Ideas' for
Cornford's 'Forms'. His 'Kinds' are γένη, a word which Taylor
(*op. cit.* p. 389) says is 'used interchangeably' with εἴδη but which
could have more than an etymological connection with our 'genera'.

comprehended within a single genus. Then, when he has reached that stage, he starts on the complementary process of Division, to corroborate, modify or refute the previous Collection. Presumably, therefore, the second and even more obscure half of the sentence goes on to describe the results of the ensuing Division. If the Collection has been accurate, and the correct genus chosen, the Division will bring to light all the essential characteristics that distinguish one constituent species from another. Each species will thus be seen to be a complex (or 'whole') of those essential characteristics, and the dialectician will now understand rationally, what before he had only discerned by intuition, how a single generic Idea does unite its many constituent sub-genera and species into an intelligible hierarchy.

An obvious illustration of Plato's dialectical method in terms of modern counterparts would be a classificatory table, in a textbook of zoology, of the *summum genus* Animal. Such a table might begin with the primary dichotomy into Vertebrate and Invertebrate and end at the indivisible species. Platonic Dialectic is indeed, as has been said earlier, the prototype of modern scientific classification. But there are two radical differences.

The first difference, which is admirably brought out in Cornford's book *Plato's Theory of Knowledge* (pp. 268–71), might almost be inferred from the passage just considered. To Aristotle, as presumably to the average modern zoologist, the most real things in the world are the particular specimens of a natural species—individual men or horses, for example—which he called 'primary substances'.

Specific concepts, such as the species Duck-billed Platypus or Siamese Cat,[1] are not for Aristotle full-blooded realities with an independent existence of their own; though still important to him, they are secondary in status. And the further we ascend in the hierarchy of species and genera the further we are going from reality. To Aristotle, in a word, you and I are the realities; the species Man is less real, being to some extent an abstraction; Biped is less real still and Animal far removed from reality. Plato's scale of reality is the exact reverse. The further we ascend from particulars to what Aristotle regarded as abstractions, the greater for Plato the reality.

The other difference involves turning on to the passage in the *Sophist* that follows almost immediately. At 254 b 7 the Stranger returns from his brief digression on dialectic and continues as follows (with slight revisions to Cornford's translation):

Now that we are agreed, then, that some of the Kinds will combine with one another and some will not, and that some combine to a small extent, others with a large number, while some pervade all and there is nothing against their being combined with everything, let us next follow up the argument in this way. We will not take all the Ideas, for fear of getting confused in such a multitude, but choose out some of those that are recognized as most important, and consider first their several natures and then how they stand in respect of being capable of combination with one another. . . . Now, among the Kinds, those we were just now discussing—Existence itself and Rest and Motion—*are* most important.

[1] These examples are less frivolous than they may sound. More obvious illustrations such as Horse fail because they are further divisible.

And a few lines further on he adds the Ideas of Sameness and Difference.

To pursue the argument of the *Sophist* further would only confuse the issue, since it is no longer concerned with dialectic. But this last brief excerpt deserves careful consideration. A noteworthy point is that what the Stranger here calls 'the most important Kinds' figured also in the final excerpt from the *Parmenides* quoted in the last chapter. That passage listed five pairs of opposite concepts: One and Plurality, Likeness and Unlikeness (or Sameness and Difference), Rest and Motion, Being (or Existence) and Not-Being, Coming-to-be and Perishing. Each member of each of these pairs, according to the advice of the old Parmenides to the young Socrates, had to be hypothesized in turn and all its consequences thoroughly examined. Such was the 'preliminary training' necessary to the proper understanding and justification of the Ideas themselves. When, therefore, the Stranger of the *Sophist* refers to Existence, Rest and Motion, Sameness and Difference as 'some of the Ideas that are recognized as most important', we can assume with fair confidence that he had in mind also the others listed in the *Parmenides*.

But from the *Sophist* there emerges clearly enough a new notion that was not altogether apparent from the *Parmenides*. The whole passage just considered has been concerned with the hierarchical arrangement of the Ideas, and it has prescribed as the task of the true philosopher, or dialectician, the study of the way in which the higher, wider, generic Ideas pervade the lower, narrower, specific Ideas. The generic Idea Animal is wider and higher than the specific Ideas Man and Horse, and therefore richer and more real. But here, suddenly, we pass to highest and broadest Ideas, 'those that are recognized as most important', and the Stranger goes on to show how three of the five selected, namely Existence, Sameness and Difference, are all-pervading, while the other two, Motion and Rest, divide all between them. The conclusion seems inevitable. Dialectic, the process of Collection and Division of Ideas, brings us sooner or later up to this all-pervading level of reality. With the solitary exception of the Idea of the Good in the *Republic*, which was said to lie beyond even Being, these are the highest, most comprehensive and richest realities we have or could have encountered. This is where the progressive Collections of higher and higher generic Ideas will eventually lead us, and from here the complementary Divisions will lead us down again, step by step through ever narrower and lower Ideas, to the lowest levels of reality, the indivisible species. To descend beyond that to the particular is no part of the business of dialectic. A far cry indeed from modern science.

The processes involved in this extraordinary intellectual exercise are nowhere more fully or clearly described than in the passages quoted from the *Phaedrus* and the *Sophist*. The *Statesman* admittedly adds a little, but how little can be seen from the following succinct summary of its contribution by Ross (*Plato's Theory of Ideas*, p. 118):

Two important principles with regard to the world of Ideas are here recognized. One is that its structure is a stratified structure. The division of mankind into Greeks and barbarians is bad because it ignores this principle; the Greeks are 'too small a chip' of the whole, not on the same level of generality as the class with which they are contrasted. In dividing, we should not pass direct from 'man' to 'Greek', but recognize the intervening classes. The second principle is that the absence of a positive characteristic does not in itself constitute a class. A barbarian, for a Greek, was simply one who was not a Greek; 'barbarian' was as negative a term as 'not-ten-thousand' would be.

The first principle, which is very important, has already emerged from the *Sophist*. The second, however valuable (and its relevance to the dichotomy Vertebrate–Invertebrate is noteworthy), concerns so special an aspect of the science of dialectic that it throws little light on the whole. However closely Plato's collected works are studied, they will never yield a detailed picture of his dialectical method and many of the most interesting questions will for ever remain unanswered. To the end of his life he adhered to the decision enunciated in the passage already quoted from the *Republic*. Socrates, urged to 'describe the function of dialectic, into what divisions it falls and what are its methods', replies: 'My dear Glaucon, you will not be able to follow me further, though not for want of willingness on my part. It would mean that, instead of illustrating the truth by an allegory, I should be showing you the truth itself, at least as it appears to me.' So the *Sophist*, though its description of the dialectical method gives us more to go on than any other passage from Plato, is proved to be regrettably fragmentary by the single fact that, far as it ascends through the hierarchy of Ideas, it contains no mention of the Idea of the Good nor any suggestion of a substitute for it. Yet there must surely be something to co-ordinate the *summa genera* of the *Sophist* into an all-embracing unity, and on that fundamental question Plato saw fit to be less informative to posterity in writing than he doubtless was by word of mouth to his colleagues and pupils.

The later dialectic, according to the majority of scholars, replaced rather than amplified the conception of it put forward in the *Republic*. The paragraph just quoted from Ross's book *Plato's Theory of Ideas* is followed at once by an equally succinct conclusion:

It will be seen that the conception of dialectic, i.e. of philosophy, put forward in the *Phaedrus, the Sophistes,* and the *Politicus* [*Statesman*] is quite different from that put forward in the *Republic*. The objective of dialectic is no longer to deduce all truth from a single transcendent truth. It is a more modest and a more realizable one—one with which Plato at least succeeds in making a beginning—that of tracing the relations of assertability and deniability that exist between Ideas, and the relations of genus and species that exist between them. It is typical of Aristotle's good sense that, while he completely rejected the ideal of deducing all truth from a single truth, he accepted from Plato the notions of genus, species and differentia,and by adding to them the natural corollaries, property and accident, established his doctrine of predicables.

This pithy paragraph was written by the most eminent of all recent students of Aristotle. Everybody would agree that in formalizing and systematizing the numerous notions which Plato chose to throw out haphazard Aristotle showed the greatest good sense. Many students of Plato, however, will feel a pang of regret, to which Aristotelians may be immune, at the passing of the single transcendental truth. Both lines of thought had, of course, the profoundest influence. The earlier led on, for instance, to Plotinus and the Cambridge Platonists; the later, through Aristotle himself, who was Plato's pupil for almost twenty years, to Thomas Aquinas. And the earlier, though notably absent from the *Parmenides* and the *Sophist*, makes a final reappearance in the *Timaeus*, Plato's mythical account of the creation of the world.

Plato himself does not claim literal truth for the discourse that he puts into the mouth of the probably fictitious Timaeus of Locri.

If, Socrates [he makes him say at 29c4], in many respects concerning many things—the gods and the generation of the universe—we prove unable to render an account at all points entirely consistent with itself and exact, you must not be surprised. If we can furnish accounts no less likely than any other, we must be content, remembering that I who speak and you my judges are only human, and consequently it is fitting that we should, in these matters, accept the likely story and look for nothing further.

For, as he has already explained (28a1), 'that which is apprehensible by thought with a rational account is the thing that is always unchangeably real; whereas that which is the object of belief together with unreasoning sensation is the thing that becomes and passes away, but never has real being'. The Ideas are always unchangeably real; the world is the object of belief and sensation, has no real being and at best therefore permits only of a likely story.

Let us, then [Timaeus goes on], state for what reason becoming and this universe were framed by him who framed them.

He was good; and in the good no jealousy in any matter can ever arise. So, being without jealousy, he desired that all things should come as near as possible to being like himself. . . . Desiring, then, that all things should be good and, so far as might be, nothing imperfect, the god took over all that is visible—not at rest, but in discordant and unordered motion— and brought it from disorder into order, since he judged that order was in every way the better.

Now it was not, nor can it ever be, permitted that the work of the supremely good should be anything but that which is best. Taking thought, therefore, he found that, among things that are by nature visible, no work that is without intelligence will ever be better than one that has intelligence . . . and moreover that intelligence cannot be present in anything apart from soul. In virtue of this reasoning, when he framed the universe, he fashioned reason within soul and soul within body. . . . This, then, is how we must say, according to the likely account, that this world came to be, by the god's providence, in very truth a living creature with soul and reason.

These passages, all from the first three pages of Timaeus' discourse, introduce at once the chief peculiarities of Plato's version of the creation. The most striking feature is that the divine craftsman who framed the universe, the so-called Demiurge, is not in the normal sense of the word a Creator at all. He did not create the world of Ideas, 'the thing that is always unchangeably real', but, as Timaeus goes on to explain, used it as his model; nor did he create matter, but 'took over all that is visible—not at rest, but in discordant and unordered motion—and brought it from disorder into order'. The way in which he saw fit to do that was, as we soon learn, to mould matter into the likeness of 'that Living Creature of which all other living creatures, severally and in their families, are parts'. Hence the world is 'in very truth a living creature with soul and reason'.

The next three pages of the dialogue, concerned with the body of the world, are scarcely relevant. But at 34 b 10 Timaeus passes to the World-Soul and says that 'though it comes later in the account we are now attempting . . . the god made soul prior to body and more venerable in birth and excellence, to be the body's mistress and governor'. And he then goes on, in a sentence which Cornford calls 'one of the most obscure in the whole dialogue' (*Plato's Cosmology*, p. 59) and is reduced to breaking up into four parts, to describe the World-Soul's composition:

The things of which he composed soul and the manner of its composition were as follows: (1) Between the indivisible Existence that is ever in the same state and the divisible Existence that becomes in bodies, he compounded a third form of Existence composed of both. (2) Again, in the case of Sameness and in that of Difference, he also on the same principle made a compound intermediate between that kind of them which is indivisible and the kind that is divisible in bodies. (3) Then, taking the three, he blended them all into a unity, forcing the nature of Difference, hard as it was to mingle, into union with Sameness, and mixing them together with Existence.

Nobody could deny the obscurity of that passage, which is indeed quoted partly as an illustration of the complexity of much of Plato's later thought. But the sentence is interesting for other reasons too. As Cornford later says (*op. cit.* p. 61), 'the terms Existence, Sameness, Difference would be simply unintelligible to anyone who had not read and understood the *Sophist*', which is a powerful justification for regarding the *Timaeus* as the later of the two. And even more important, it tells us, in however obscure a fashion, that the soul is in its nature intermediate between Ideas and particulars, partaking of both Being and becoming. What Plato had written long ago in the *Phaedo* is still true for him: 'The soul is most like the divine, immortal, intelligible, simple and indissoluble.' But in the *Timaeus* the doctrine is elaborated by what Plato had even earlier called 'thinking out the reason why'. Added to the doctrine of the *Phaedrus*, which is repeated in the *Laws*, that 'the essence and definition of soul is self-motion', it reveals that Plato had in the end accepted soul as the link that he had long been seeking between the world of Ideas and the world of sense. For human souls contain the same basic ingredients as the World-Soul, even if compounded in a less pure mixture and further contaminated by the mortal elements of 'dread and necessary affections: first pleasure, the strongest lure of evil; next, pains that take flight from good; temerity moreover and fear, a pair of unwise counsellors; passion hard to entreat, and hope too easily led astray' (69 c 8).

At 44 d 3 Timaeus proceeds to the construction of the human body which is to house the immortal soul, and thereafter the greater part of the dialogue is devoted to Plato's peculiar brand of anatomy, physiology, physics and chemistry. The effect of much of it is bizarre rather than illuminating, as the opening paragraph will show:

Copying the round shape of the universe, they [the gods to whom the Demiurge had delegated the task of creating mortal things] confined the two divine revolutions in a spherical body—the head, as we now call it—which is the divinest part of us and lord over all the rest. To this the gods gave the whole body, when they had assembled it, for its service, perceiving that it possessed all the motions that were to be. Accordingly, that the head might not roll upon the ground with its heights and hollows of all sorts, and have no means to surmount the one or to climb out of the other, they gave it the body as a vehicle for ease of travel; that is why the body is elongated and grew four limbs that can be stretched out or bent, the god contriving thus for its travelling. Clinging and supporting itself with these limbs, it is able to make its way through every region, carrying at the top of us the habitation of the most divine and sacred part. Thus and for these reasons legs and arms grew upon us all. And the gods, holding that the front is more honourable and fit to lead than the back, gave us movement for the most part in that direction. So man must needs have the front of the body distinguished and unlike the back; so first they set the face on the globe of the head on that side and fixed in it organs for all the forethought of the soul, and appointed this, our natural front, to be the part having leadership.

Plato had made an unconscious contribution to science by his invention of classification. His conscious contributions are all alike permeated by the teleology that is so marked a feature here. But Plato was scarcely a born scientist. Aristotle was: his biological treatises reveal him as an exceptionally acute observer. Yet even Aristotle's theory is to a large extent invalidated by the teleological outlook which he certainly shared with his master and had presumably inherited from him.

At 47e3, however, when Plato passes in the central section of the dialogue to describe what he calls Necessity and its effects, he momentarily deserts science and reverts to first principles. The opening sentences of the section are, as all commentators have recognized with widely divergent results, of crucial importance for the interpretation not only of the *Timaeus* but of Plato's metaphysics and theology as a whole. This is how they run:

Now our foregoing discourse, save for a few matters, has set forth the works wrought by the craftsmanship of reason; but we must now set beside them the things that come about of Necessity. For the generation of the universe was a mixed result of the combination of Necessity and Reason. Reason overruled Necessity by persuading her to guide the greatest part of the things that become towards what is best; in that way and on that principle this universe was fashioned in the beginning by the victory of reasonable persuasion over Necessity. If, then, we are really to tell how it came into being on this principle, we must bring in also the Errant Cause —in what manner its nature is to cause motion. So we must return on our steps thus, and taking, in its turn, a second principle concerned in the origin of these same things, start once more upon our present theme from the beginning.

This paragraph raises, in an acute form, the few questions still to be discussed. Did Plato really believe in a divine Creator, hardly distinguishable from the Creator of the Book of Genesis? If so, is that Creator to be identified with the Idea of the Good in the *Republic* or what otherwise is the relation between the two? And finally, if the world was really the product of 'the combination of Necessity and Reason', which between them should

surely be capable of attaining perfection, then why is the
world so very imperfect and what is the explanation of
evil? Almost every imaginable answer has before now
been given to each of these questions and some of the
answers are demonstrably wrong. But to decide which is
the right answer is not a simple task.

The first question is the easiest of the three but still
difficult to answer with a straight Yes or No. Plato tried
in the *Timaeus* to do exactly what he had represented
Socrates in the *Phaedo* as unable to do, namely to discover,
by studying particulars, how everything was arranged, as
it should be, in the best possible way. His account of the
creation of the universe is only, by his own admission,
'no less likely than any other'. It is, in other words, not
so much a description of an event in time as an analysis
of the world and its contents as we find them. The Demiurge, who merely took over, rather than brought into
existence, both the material on which he had to work and
the model whose perfection he was attempting to reproduce in space, represents the orderly, predictable and
therefore fully intelligible element in the world-order.
Despite numerous attempts to prove his omnipotence,
Plato's Demiurge, represented in this last passage by
Reason, is as much restricted as the human craftsman to
whom he is likened by the intransigence of the materials
on which he has to work. The Creator in the Book of
Genesis had only to speak the word and what he willed
was instantly forthcoming. Plato's Demiurge had a
harder task. He had to persuade Necessity 'to guide the
greatest part of the things that become towards what is

best'. Had Plato wished to say, as many commentators have suggested that he did, that Necessity stands merely for those links in the chain of cause and effect which we do not yet understand, that it is ultimately subject to the will of the Creator and that it represents therefore nothing more than the method by which that Creator chose to impose order on chaos, why should he have described Reason as 'persuading' (rather than coercing) 'the greatest part of the things that become' (rather than all of them) 'towards what is best'? Many supporting arguments could be adduced, but this one alone is enough to dispose of the equation of Plato's Demiurge with Jehovah or Almighty God.

The answer to the first question has partly answered the second as well. If the Demiurge is a mythical figure, simply symbolizing the rational element in the universe, then the question what is his relation to the Idea of the Good is misguided. Every Idea is, in the *Timaeus* as in earlier dialogues, a separate part of 'the thing that is always unchangeably real'. The Demiurge is no more than the leading character in a 'likely story'. The *Timaeus*, so far from replacing Plato's earlier metaphysics with a monotheism that anticipates Christianity, is yet one more elaborate attempt to forge a link between Being, or Ideas, and becoming, or the particulars of the sensible world. For though once again the Idea of the Good is in the *Timaeus* conspicuous by its absence, not only the Idea of Living Creature in whose image the world was fashioned, and the generic and specific Ideas comprehended within it, but also the Ideas of Fire, Air, Water and Earth (briefly but unhesitatingly accepted at 51 b–e), show beyond any doubt that Plato is still basing his entire philosophy, his cosmology included, on the hypothesis of the Ideas.

The *Timaeus* then, to pass to the final question, sets up yet again the two worlds, the ideal and the sensible, and yet again seeks for the connection between them. Not for the first or last time it seems to find that connection in soul. But the new conception of Necessity is an urgently needed addition to the theory of Ideas. Those who come unprepared to the thought and writings of the greatest of Greek philosophers may find this new conception paradoxical if not baffling. For both Plato and Aristotle, Necessity was not, as it is to us, the mechanical and invariable law that a given cause produces a given effect. It was rather the spontaneous, the unpredictable and, above all, the purposeless; roughly what we call Chance. This is the element in the eternal material given by Plato to his Demiurge which Reason has to overrule, and the fact that Reason succeeded in persuading it only 'to guide the greatest part of the things that become towards what is best' accounts for the evil and the pain that the world contains.

So, in the last resort, the gulf between the two worlds remains flimsily bridged. Like Eros in the *Symposium*, soul in the *Timaeus* is intermediate in status between them; as valid an answer, perhaps, as any yet given to the problem of the relationship between the eternal and the temporal. But the details of that relationship remained for Plato, as they have for most others, an open question till the end of his life.

SELECTIVE BIBLIOGRAPHY

The following list, which I have kept as short as possible, is for the benefit of non-specialists. It includes only a few of the most useful books, or parts of books, which are written in English and demand little or no knowledge of Greek; it excludes all articles from learned journals; it consists primarily of fuller expositions of the topics discussed in this essay, and for that reason omits many valuable studies of aspects of Platonic philosophy other than the metaphysical. All the authors to whose books I have referred in the text are of course listed in the General Index.

I should like to thank the Cambridge University Press for allowing me to quote from R. Hackforth's translations from Plato, and the Clarendon Press and Messrs Routledge and Kegan Paul for allowing me to quote from F. M. Cornford's translations, as noted in the text.

GENERAL WORKS ON PLATO

CORNFORD, F. M. *Before and after Socrates* (Cambridge University Press, 1932).

CROMBIE, I. M. *An Examination of Plato's Doctrines* (Routledge and Kegan Paul, vol. I, 1962; vol. II, 1963).

FIELD, G. C. *Plato and his Contemporaries* (Methuen, 1930).

GRUBE, G. M. A. *Plato's Thought* (Methuen, 1935).

ROBINSON, R. *Plato's Earlier Dialectic* (Clarendon Press, 2nd ed. 1953).

ROSS, W. D. (Sir DAVID). *Plato's Theory of Ideas* (Clarendon Press, 1951).

STEWART, J. A. *The Myths of Plato* (Macmillan, 1905)—included only because it contains all the myths in translation.

TAYLOR, A. E. *Plato: The Man and his Work* (Methuen, 3rd ed. 1929).

SELECTIVE BIBLIOGRAPHY

TRANSLATIONS AND/OR COMMENTARIES
ON PARTICULAR WORKS

CORNFORD, F. M. *The 'Republic' of Plato* (Clarendon Press, 1941).

—*Plato and Parmenides* (Routledge and Kegan Paul, 1939).

—*Plato's Theory of Knowledge* (Routledge and Kegan Paul, 1935).

—*Plato's Cosmology* (Routledge and Kegan Paul, 1937).

HACKFORTH, R. *The Authorship of the Platonic Epistles* (Manchester University Press, 1913).

—*Plato's 'Phaedo'* (Cambridge University Press, 1955).

—*Plato's 'Phaedrus'* (Cambridge University Press, 1952).

NETTLESHIP, R. L. *Lectures on the 'Republic' of Plato* (Macmillan, 1898).

SKEMP, J. B. *Plato's 'Statesman'* (Routledge and Kegan Paul, 1952).

INTRODUCTIONS, NOTES OR APPENDICES
TO EDITIONS OF A GREEK TEXT

ADAM, J. *Plato, 'Protagoras'* (Cambridge University Press, 1893).

—*The 'Republic' of Plato* (Cambridge University Press, 1902).

BLUCK, R. S. *Plato's 'Meno'* (Cambridge University Press, 1961).

BURY, R. G. *Plato, The 'Symposium'* (Cambridge University Press, 1909).

DODDS, E. R. *Plato, 'Gorgias'* (Clarendon Press, 1959).

ROSS, W. D. (Sir David). *Aristotle's 'Metaphysics'* (Clarendon Press, 1924).

INDEX OF PASSAGES QUOTED
FROM PLATO

GENERAL INDEX

abstraction (διάνοια), state of mind corresponding to 'unco-ordinated Ideas' (CE) segment in analogy of Divided Line, 153, 163; intermediate between intelligence and belief, 162–3; induced by study of mathematics, 180–1

Academy, the, discussions at, 25, 217; Plato as head of, 31, 73–5, 203; pupils at, 32, 39; foundation of, 55, 69, 71–3

Adam, J., Plato, 'Protagoras' by, 47, 48, 245; The 'Republic' of Plato by, 142, 143, 149, 156, 165, 171, 245

Adeimantus, Plato's brother, 27; in the Republic, 121

Aegina, Plato saved from slavery at, 72–3

aesthetics, doctrine of Ideas and, (Symp.) 75, (Phaedo) 96, 101

ἀγάπη, St Paul's word for love, 109

Agathon, tragedian, in the Symposium, 110–11

Alcibiades, 31; in the Symposium, 106

Anaxagoras, on Mind as moving cause, 87, 88, 89

Anaximander, Milesian philosopher, 1

Anaximenes, Milesian philosopher, 1

Anniceris, ransoms Plato from Spartans, 72–3

Antiphon, Plato's half-brother, 27

Apology, 9, 41, 43; dating of, 35; apparent agnosticism of, 68

Archytas of Tarentum, Pythagorean, 69, 206

Aristo, Plato's father, 27

Aristophanes, in the Symposium, 108

Aristophanes of Byzantium, arrangement of Plato's works by, 20

Aristotle, on Plato's debt to Pythagoras and Heraclitus, 4, 5, 10; Metaphysics by, 5, 10, 36, 39, 83, 155; on Ideas of Plato, 11, 39, 40–1, 213, 214, 216, 223; on Universals of Socrates, 11, 39, 83–4, 125; Politics by, 33; pupil of Plato, 39, 75, 235; development of dialectic by, 96; on Intermediates, 155; on Prime Mover, 196; on Plato's Unwritten Doctrines, 224 n.; scale of reality of, 229–30; doctrine of predicables of, 234; teleological outlook of, 239; attitude of, to Necessity, 243

arithmetic, in education of Guardians, 178

Art, chosen as summum genus for Angler, (Soph.) 225

astronomy, studied by Pythagoras, 4; in education of Guardians (as branch of mathematics), 178–80, 181

Athens, Plato and, 27, 28, 31, 32, 52, 73, 204, 207

atomic theory, of Leucippus and Democritus, 7

'attunement' or 'harmony' theory of the soul, 82–3

Beauty, absolute, (Symp.) 107, 109, 113–16; education for recognition of, (Rep.) 121–3

Being and Not-being, see Existence and Non-existence

belief (opinion), concerned with Things (as knowledge with Ideas), 4, 7, 64, 70, 137–8, 166, 172, 235; converted to knowledge by 'thinking out the reason why', (Meno) 65, 68, 127, 238; education for rightness of, (Rep.) 122, 126–7, 177; state of mind corresponding to 'Things' (DC) segment in analogy of Divided Line, 163